GESTALT THERAPY and BEYOND

An Integrated Mind-Body Approach

ERIC H. MARCUS, M. D.

A Publication of The Gestalt Journal Press

This book was originally published by Meta Publications in 1979 and is reprinted here by arrangement with the author.

Published by:

The Gestalt Journal Press, Inc.
A Division of:
The Center for Gestalt Development, Inc.
P. O. Box 278
Gouldsboro ME 04607-0278
U.S.A.

ISBN 978-0-939266-48-7

ACKNOWLEDGEMENTS

I wish to express my appreciation to Jenny Gumpertz, whose editorial work has patiently and skillfully guided my efforts during the past several years. I also appreciate Silvia R. Marcus for offering her perceptive critique of my manuscript. I am especially grateful to John Stevens for his efforts at reviewing the completed manuscript and making detailed comments and critique—some of which has been included in the text. I am also grateful to Richard Ferman, M.D., who originally suggested that I write this book.

CONTENTS

PREFACE

In the 15th and 16th centuries, Dutch, Portuguese, Spanish and English mariners ventured forth on voyages of discovery. Many of these voyages were financed by the governments of those countries and had as their primary objective the discovery of maritime routes which led to parts of the world where unusual (for occidentals) products, herbs, spices, perfumes, etc. were available for trade. The governments of those nations understood clearly that charted, mapped, reliable routes to heretofore undiscovered civilizations or routes to previously contacted civilizations which were more reliable, shorter or safer than previously discovered routes would give the finders of such routes domination in trade with their competitors. Each of the various competing nations entered the contest with different attitudes, personnel and ships. Some of the ships involved sacrificed stability for speed—others, robustness for precision. Initially in this intensely competitive era, the most widely recognized and closely guarded of objects which gave its possessor the critical advantage in this contest was the rutter—a personal log religiously kept by the pilot/navigator on these voyages of discovery. Later in the heat of competition, blatant open military warfare (e.g., the English/Spanish sea battles in the Carribean) succeeded the development of reliable rutters as the primary technique of gaining the competitive edge each of these nations sought. But it is to the earlier form—the rutter—and its era that I direct the reader's attention.

As James Clavell expressed it in his epic historical novel *Shogun* (p. 11):

> "A rutter was a small book containing the detailed observation of a pilot *who had been there before.* It recorded magnetic compass courses between ports and capes, headlands and channels. It noted the sounding and depths and color of the water and the nature of the seabed. It set down the *how we got there and how we got back;* how many days on a special tack, the pattern of the wind, when it blew and from where, what currents to expect and from where; the time of storms and the time of fair winds; where to careen the ship and where to water; where there were friends and where foes; shoals, reefs, tides, havens; at best, *everything* necessary for a safe voyage.
>
> The English, Dutch, and French had rutters for their own waters, but the waters of the rest of the world had been sailed only by captains from Portugal and Spain, and these two countries considered all rutters secret. Rutters that revealed the seaways to the New World or unraveled the mysteries of the Pass of Magellan and the Cape of Good Hope—both Portuguese discoveries—and thence the seaways to Asia were guarded as national treasures by the Portuguese and Spanish, and sought after with equal ferocity by their Dutch and English enemies."

The rutter then was a chronicle of a voyage—a series of sensory grounded descriptions which could be used as a guide to travel safely and efficiently to a destination and back again. As Clavell points out, " . . . a rutter was only as good as the pilot who wrote it . . . " Different pilots had differing abilities to detect and record the various aspects of their adventure. Thus even when in possession of a rutter from a pilot who had created it during a specific voyage of discovery, a pilot never knew whether the rutter was adequate for certain until he *had been there himself.*

In the 19th and 20th centuries, one of the more challenging of the voyages of discovery is that involved with the largely uncharted and turbulant water of the inner sea. And while the names of the destinations sought by the mariners of the previous era differ from the names of the typical destinations of our modern adventures, the sense of wonder, alertness and courage in approaching such unknowns still characterizes this activity when successful, and of similar great importances are the observations of our modern navigators. I leave you now in the hands of the good pilot, Eric Marcus.

John Grinder
January, 1979
Ben Lomond, California

INTRODUCTION

Eric—

I want to share the image that I had while reading your book. I saw you sitting in front of a giant T.V. screen which showed a continual stream of ways in which human beings can get unstuck and go on with their growing. You appeared relaxed and interested as each direction presented itself. Periodically you would step in, emphasizing some points, disagreeing with others, and then making a relevant application drawn from your own experience which would serve to highlight both your criticisms and emphases. The finished product was actually a process of weeding, sorting, combining and connecting the parts relevant to you and your way of viewing things. This gave me a spiritual-like, round feeling about how you build, which can be very useful for any therapist as he or she wades into the mass of material currently available regarding change in human beings.

Actually your work represents a monumental effort which left me, the reader, the feeling that there is much more to come. I personally like things that are process-oriented and do not look only to an end point. This book should be of interest to every therapist.

Virginia M. Satir
Menlo Park, California
January 1979

Chapter I

THEORETICAL AND CLINICAL

GESTALT THERAPY AND BEYOND

Eric H. Marcus, M.D.

Gestalt therapy and methodology form the basic core of my work as a therapist. But during the past few years I have moved away from gestalt as an exclusive modality and have incorporated certain other therapy systems and techniques. I have tended to combine whichever approaches are the most likely to involve both the mind and the body in an integrated way. I came to this position by evolution, by discovering what was missing in "conventional" gestalt therapy. So my basic orientation is the existential, nonanalytic, process-oriented approach of gestalt. But even though gestalt is amazingly effective in its use of the body as a projective device, it offers no methods of direct work on body armor. Reichian and Neo-Reichian methods do provide this direct body contact and actually loosen the muscular armoring; however, they frequently do not involve cognitive processes. I've found that guided imagery is effective in integrating mind-body work, at both superficial and deep levels. And psychodramatic methods have offered my clients an active bodily involvement in the process of discovery and growth. My personal approach, therefore, has become a blending of gestalt with Neo-Reichian, guided imagery, and psychodramatic methods, to involve both the mind and the body in the therapeutic process.

So I would like to share some of my views of gestalt therapy and describe my process of incorporating other methods into my system. Since gestalt therapy is no longer in its infancy, a number of books have appeared since Fritz Perls' first writings. It would be redundant to present a lengthy elaboration of basic gestalt philosophy and methodology. Instead, I want to *extend* the understanding of these principles through extensive use of transcripts of work sessions, which will appear in later chapters, accompanied by discussions of the principles being illustrated. I hope that this approach will clarify the nature of the gestalt experience more effectively than discussions *about* gestalt therapy.

First, I want to emphasize that there is a substantial distinction between gestalt philosophy and gestalt methodology. One can subscribe to gestalt philosophy and never use gestalt methodology, and vice versa. Gestalt *philosophy* refers to certain principles of existential living. Gestalt *methodology* consists of the technical implementation of these principles in psychotherpy settings and elsewhere.

The essentials of gestalt philosophy are best conveyed in the brief and straightforward manner set forth by Claudio Naranjo in *Gestalt Therapy Now.* These nine principles are neither unique nor original. In fact, all of them can be found in ancient writings such as the Bible, Koran and Zen scriptures. Through gestalt techniques the client can learn to live consistently with these principles.

Principle 1—"Live now. Be concerned with the present rather than with the past or future."

Principle 2—"Live here. Deal with what is present rather than with what is absent."

Principle 3—"Stop imagining. Experience the real."

Principle 4—"Stop unnecessary thinking. Rather, taste and see."

Principle 5—"Express rather than manipulate, explain, justify, or judge."

Principle 6—"Give in to unpleasantness and pain just as to pleasure."

Principle 7—"Accept no should or ought other than your own. Adore no graven image."

Principle 8—"Take full responsibility for your actions, feelings, and thoughts."

Principle 9—"Surrender to being as you are."

Gestalt methodology includes therapy practices that are generally associated with gestalt—for example, the "empty chair" technique and doing "rounds." Attending a few gestalt workshops or learning some potent gestalt techniques does not make one a gestalt therapist. But the techniques can be a valuable supplement to a wide variety of therapeutic approaches, without the therapist necessarily obtaining an understanding of basic gestalt philosophy.

Gestalt methodology can be considered in three parts: *contact*, *process* and *experimentation.*

Contact. The nature of a client's contact with the therapist elicits a wealth of therapeutic material. The client relates to the therapist both as a real person and as a transference figure. As a "real" person, the therapist (knowingly or not) serves as a model for behavior. The therapeutic transaction deals with the manner of the relationship between the therapist and client, which inevitably includes the client's neurotic manipulations and other characteristics of his life script.

Process. A second characteristic of gestalt therapy is the therapist's almost continuous attention to "process." Process refers to *how* the client does what he does. The client's usual focus is on the content of the material he is presenting, but most of the client's resistances are manifest in the process itself. The therapist directs the client's awareness to his process at appropriate times.

Awareness is the sine qua non of the gestalt process. Awareness is attention to what *is* happening (rather than what *was* or *will be*), whether in the therapeutic situation or in the client's life. Only when awareness exists can the client realize that choices also exist. Which choice to make (or the choice to make no choices) is up to the client rather than the therapist.

Experimentation. The third and perhaps uniquely gestalt feature is the use of experiments. Experiments are opportunities to behave/feel/think differently within the safe confines of a therapy situation. For me one of the most enjoyable aspects of being a gestalt therapist is tapping my creativity to design experiments for clients.

Gradually I began to incorporate techniques drawn from other systems of therapy. I knew that this eclectic approach made sense, but it was not jelled in my mind as a philosophy until I went to a workshop with psychologist Paul Bindrim and heard his theoretical presentation of the process of psychotherapy and growth. When I used his scheme, then a variety of approaches such as gestalt, meditation and psychedelics seemed to fit together.

Bindrim considers the personality as a series of concentric circles, the outermost circle representing a person's defenses, including their "character," in the sense of a fixed way of being, a lifestyle, a life script—synonymous with "character armor" or "character defenses."

Underneath this outermost layer lie painful and strong emotions. In gestalt we define four basic emotions: anger, joy, grief and orgasm, although I really don't think these are necessarily the only basic ones. The first three are commonly expressed in therapy; most of us don't deal directly with orgasms. In my opinion, most therapies—gestalt included—don't go further than this second layer, and many therapies don't even get to strong feelings.

I have been using Neo-Reichian and bioenergetic techniques to get persons in touch with strong emotions very quickly. However, sometimes these methods work almost too fast. People pass through character defenses quickly and discharge strong emotions, but they may revert back to their original defenses. On the other hand, therapists who never facilitate clients' getting in touch with strong emotions keep therapy at a predominantly intellectual level. I favor a combination of approaches, that is, facilitating powerful emotional expression and then integrating the experience by means of gestalt therapy.

Somehow I had suspected that these two layers were not an adequate conceptualization of a total being. I still had no clear concept as to what was the next level down until I went to Bindrim's lecture. He called level three "aloneness," the process of getting in touch with actually being totally alone, having no real outside support in life. It is the place where we know that no one will live for us and nobody will die for us. This realization is a very frightening gut feeling. Very few therapies touch on this level, and there aren't many techniques available to elicit it. One such technique is isolation. At the Gestalt Institute of Canada, people used to stay alone in a cabin for one month. They could get as much therapy as they wanted, but when they were not in therapy, they were to remain alone. Janov has people stay a week or two alone in a motel in order to get in touch with aloneness as well as to let go of defenses. I think that isolation is a fast way of getting down to these deeper levels.

At the center of Bindrim's concentric circles is "fusion" or "love"—the place representing complete centeredness. This, of course, is an ideal—at least a place we reach only sometimes. Most of us don't have the kind of lifestyle that makes such an existence possible. In Zen philosophy this place is called the state of Zen, where we "merge" with the universe. There are very few people who can reach this level and who can also move in and out of it. And yet some people do reach it by a variety of methods—psychotherapy is perhaps an inefficient one. Far more efficient are drugs such as LSD, meditation, including Yoga, Zen and Transcendental Meditation. The ideal is to be able to move in and out of this place. To be there always is, I think, quite unrealistic in Western society; we still have to drive, buy groceries and make phone calls. Practically speaking it just doesn't work out to love everyone.

In terms of the psychotherapy process, we can start with clients at the outermost layer and work in toward the center, or start at the center and proceed outward. An ideal combination would be to work in both directions.

Certain therapy schools and techniques start at the superficial layer and work inward by penetrating defenses—for example, psychoanalysis, transactional analysis, Synanon games, encounter groups, and gestalt.

There are other techniques that remove defenses from the inside out. This approach is sometimes much faster and much more effective than spending years trying to break defenses from outside in. For example, massage can penetrate the center. I have attended massage workshops where some people experienced such feelings of love, security and warmth that their defenses were dissolved. Bindrim accomplishes similar releases with a more unusual technique. A group gathers in a body-temperature pool, and the participants rock and float each other in the water. Usually, within a very short time, many people have a very emotional discharge.

Another way of working from the center (which I don't use) is by administering psychedelic drugs. I am learning about the effects of LSD and mescaline from medical students and psychiatric residents whom I supervise. Most of them have had growth experiences from psychedelic drugs. I expect them to be quite a different breed of psychiatrist than my former classmates! Of course, drug trips are not integrated experiences—they are momentary flashes of insight. And yet people remember the openness and awareness they felt under these drugs and can then work toward that goal without drugs. At least the drug experience gives them a taste of something they might never have otherwise experienced, like the McDonald's patron who gets a taste of steak—and wants to eat steak again.

Members of religious groups who reach the love-fusion center suffer a particular pitfall. If they don't stay within their particular philosophical system, they may quickly revert back to their particular group, reinforced by certain chants, rituals or physical trappings. It takes many years to achieve and integrate basic personality changes in order to function in a centered way regardless of environment.

I like to provide a place where people can move into love-fusion level through contact with a warm, giving, loving group. In such a group, people are more willing to risk giving up defenses. Their defenses are melted rather than "cracked" by means of attack or group pressure. I am convinced that defenses are easier melted by love and affection than broken by harsh techniques. In fact, many growth experiences occur *outside* the therapeutic setting. Think of your own experiences. Remember your indelible moments with a good friend, spouse or teacher. The interaction with a warm, loving person (including a therapist) is the predominant healing factor, *not* the particular theory or technique of the therapist.

GESTALT THERAPY AND THE NATURE OF CHANGE

Edwin Greenberg, Ph.D.

This paper deals primarily with the nature of change. Specifically, I will speak about the gestalt position (viz., the paradoxical theory of change, a la Beisser), the classical psychoanalytic conception of change, the Rogerian position, and lastly, the Tao-Buddhistic position (which I will refer to as Zen).

Here at the beginning it is necessary to point out that a psychotherapy such as gestalt, psychoanalysis, etc., consists of considerably more than a theory of change. A psychotherapy is necessarily multidimensional in nature. In each approach to psychotherapy there is represented: (a) a theory of personality dynamics, (b) a theory of psychopathology (e.g. neurosis, psychosis), (c) a theory of defenses, (d) a metatheory about the nature of reality and how reality is apprehended (e.g., mind-body relationship), (e) a psychological energy theory and/or theory of aggression, (f) a theory of ethics, (g) a theory of change, (h) a theory of interpersonal behavior, and, (i) a style of application and technology which embodies all of the foregoing theoretical concerns.

Beisser has stated: "Change comes about when one becomes who one is and not when one tries to become what one is not." This statement of the paradoxical theory of change is predicated on four very important and fundamentally related principles. First, there is a natural self-regulating process inherent to existence—i.e. the human organism if allowed to function without constraint and interruption will take best care of itself, and will be sensitive to the needs of others as well. Second, taking care of oneself begins with taking responsibility for how one is not taking care of oneself. Third, the human organism is a phenomenon integral with its environment, and thus, peace of mind is partially a function of accepting what fate bestows upon us all including our inability to transform ourselves into our conceptualized ideals. Fourth, the human organism is capable of disowning, misapprehending, or distorting knowledge of its experience and behavior.

For many people the gestalt approach to change seems paradoxical, because people have lost faith in self-regulation, lost touch with self-responsibility. People believe they can and ought to be their ideals. So when, for example, a patient reports being anxious, and we as gestalt psychotherapists suggest that the patient get in touch with the anxiety and how he makes himself anxious, it is not uncommon for the virgin client to indicate surprise, bewilderment, and confusion. In other words, for many, change (as in the example of change from being anxious to being relaxed) logically should result from trying to make oneself less anxious, rather than being the direct and efficient result of surrendering in the now to what one is doing which produces anxiety (or in Beisser's terms, "becoming who one is").

When a therapist adopts the paradoxical theory of change, he automatically stands in opposition to what is often referred to as the medical model. The medical model presupposes an objective authority who knows what is in the best interest of the person in distress. And the function of this "objective authority" is to exorcize a pathogenic-like ingredient or mechanism *for* the client. Classical psychoanalysis was and is a psychotherapy in which the therapist adopts the medical model. It seems clear that the primary function of free association, interpretation of resistance, fixation, transference, and dreams is to disassemble the patient and then reassemble him better than the way he existed at the beginning of therapy. So, in psychoanalysis, the therapist takes major responsibility, relative to the client, for recognizing and identifying problem areas and for the restructuring of the client's personality.

Psychoanalysts were aware practically from the very beginning—from, that is, the joint work of Freud and Breuer with Anna—that the therapist did not have absolute jurisdiction over the client's experience, and that the client must cooperate and accept the here and now in order for change to occur. If the most meaningful changes in a patient's behavior result from his acceptance of what actually is, then perhaps psychoanalysis is successful to the extent that it implicitly encourages and supports this brand of self-acceptance. On the other hand, if much of psychoanalysis involves the client's replacing old and less workable introjects for the newer, more workable introjects transmitted by the therapist, change for the "better" (i.e., adjustment) may appear to occur, but not necessarily self-actualization—growth. Psychoanalysis, because it involves a considerable amount of interpretation (i.e., the whys of behavior and experience), necessarily steers the patient away from experiential ownership of the so-called pathogenic process itself, though some unsystematic ownership is likely to result in the therapeutic situation anyway.

There is also little question that the psychoanalytic view of change (i.e., change comes about as a function of understanding one's resistances and early childhood experiences) is at best neutral and most likely negative with regard to the issue of the innate goodness of human nature. In other words, working through in psychoanalysis for the avowed purpose of developing a conflict-free ego, theoretically involves sublimation of one's aggressive impulses. Therefore, changing the client within a psychoanalytic framework involves more than just developing insights, because the patient is being taught that certain natural impulses must not be expressed.

As I see it, then, there is a theme of control which runs through the psychoanalytic view of change insofar as psychoanalysis asserts a need for a strong ego to keep aggressive urges in check. And this philosophy of control runs counter to the gestalt aim of facilitating for a person the process of becoming more of who one is—some of which is probably culturally unacceptable. As I said at the beginning, a psychotherapy consists of more than a theory of change. Thus, to fully understand the differences and similarities between psychoanalysis and gestalt therapy would require much more than what I have said to this point. I hope, though, that on the basis of what has been said that some of these differences (and similarities) have emerged.

I would like now to speak about how Rogerians view the change process and contrast that with the gestalt approach. Rogerian therapy has a phenomenological basis as does gestalt therapy. By this is meant that human experience is organized in such a way that it can never be understood as a simple addition of its component parts. Rather, the natural human condition is an active process of continually emerging whole perceptions which are structured in a unique way by each organism a little differently at any moment of time, depending on the need of the moment. Thus, to understand another person is an impossibility, because complete understanding can only be found in the unique acts of being-in-the-world. The closest a phenomenologist can come to understanding another person (Rogerians claim) is through the act of empathy. That is, by adopting an attitude similar to the client's and getting a vicarious sense of how the client experiences his existence.

Rogerians work with a theory of change which, on the surface, bears similarity with the gestalt view. For a Rogerian, change comes about when the client becomes more of his actual potential and ceases trying to become an "idealized" potential which is maladaptive. However, change (i.e., from inauthenticity to authenticity) is viewed by Rogerians as primarily the result of the therapist's unconditionally accepting the client's ill-fitting behaviors and relating with him from an empathic attitude. That is, the client changes when he receives no punishment or secondary gain for his inauthenticity, and this enables the client to discriminate between what best fits his organismic experience and those false values which he has introjected. Thus, in the Rogerian system, which is predicated on an innate goodness to human nature, the inappropriate behavior will automatically cease as long as it is not reinforced, so to speak.

For me, the Rogerian approach translates into trying to become more self-accepting, or trying to become the innately good person one would have been if those conditions of worth had not developed. Gestaltists, on the other hand, do not seem interested in self-acceptance as an outcome, but rather are interested in self-acceptance as a process. The gestalt approach in effect is stating—"really be your disapproving self, sensitize yourself to what you are doing, and if you do not like the result do something different." The Rogerian on the other hand is stating—"Disapproving of self is an aberration of your true nature; you do not need to disapprove of your real self any longer and I will prove it to you by accepting you no matter what." Consequently, gestalt work focuses on getting the clients in touch with what they are doing and the Rogerians in touch with how outmoded or unnecessary their neurotic behaviors are. Further, there is an opportunity in the gestalt system for self-acceptance in everything one is doing, including self-disapproval, whereas for Rogerians self-acceptance is the result of certain cognitive acts being extinguished. Thus, gestalt can be viewed as a truer wholistic and integrated approach to change: It emphasizes self-acceptance as a process, it is more behaviorally oriented (patient acts out the disowned process), and less idyllic or value-laden than is Rogerian therapy.

At this point I want to speak about change from Taoist-Buddhistic standpoint—Zen. The fundamental axiom of Zen is that fundamentally not one separate thing exists as such. The cosmology of Zen speaks of a wholism which stupifies the reasoning mind, because the idea of "not one separate thing" runs counter to our experience of individuality. The resolution to this apparent discrepancy between our experience of individuality on the one hand and the Zen idea of no-thingness on the other bears similarity to the resolution of the gestalt paradoxical theory of change which asserts that change comes about when we become more of who we are. Zen is telling us that when a so-called individual becomes more of who he is, he becomes less of a separate thing and more of a pure process of awareness that knows and feels peace in the determinism of the moment.

The cosmology of Zen, therefore, is speaking about an environmental wholism in which intraorganismic choice is subordinate to the will of the whole. When so-called individuality yields or surrenders to its moment, experience becomes more sharply felt, but without there being a separate feeler or doer or witness to it all. Zen can easily be misunderstood to be claiming that the human condition is *confluent* with the will of the whole, but nothing could be further from what the Zen literature propounds. The experience of satori is purportedly *self*-realization in the truest phenomenological sense. Thus, satori is not the absence of a sharp figure-ground. Rather, satori is the absence of a separate evaluating witness, and it is this witnessing act which effects a reduction in the felt-definition of the figure-ground relationship. Accordingly, it is in this witnessing activity that categories of good-bad, right-wrong, top dog—bottom dog, etc., are constructed.

So, in Zen, change from ignorance to enlightenment is the phenomenological effect of a "superior" (or more realistic) gestalt formation. And this change is supposedly the immediate and automatic consequence of fully owning the witnessing activity. The Zen process of owning the witness is, as I see it, analogous to the owning process spoken about in gestalt. Owning in gestalt basically means to be fully into what is happening without a split in awareness. Similarly, owning the witness in Zen means to be fully witnessing without a witness to the witness. In so doing, theoretically, self is involved in a direct self-evident realization of the meaning of existence. And this emerges without a behind-the-scene witness, evaluating or appreciating in accordance with societally conditioned values and meanings.

Additionally, Zen tells us that our deepest innate disposition will be experienced as "perfect" when the illusion of separateness disappears. That is, we are absolutely enough, and our enoughness is realized simultaneously in owning the activity of witnessing and evaluating. In colloquial terms, the experience of "I am not enough" or "This is not enough" is "headtripping." And the absence of headtripping is correlated with peace of mind, or, to be more puristic, "peace of no mind."

In conclusion, my analysis of the Zen approach to change reveals that it adopts a paradoxical position very similar to that of gestalt therapy. Perhaps the only difference between the two disciplines is in the broader view of reality held by a particular therapist, teacher, guru, etc., who happens to be applying the paradoxical theory of change. Typically for a Zen Master, the pragmatic question of how change comes about is not independent of the answer to the questions, "How is reality apprehended?" "What is the nature of reality?" and "Can reality know us?" I feel assured that every therapist adopts a position (usually without awareness) in regard to these questions. And if change and the nature of reality are integral with each other, it is essential that the therapist examine more closely his metaphysical framework. Perhaps the wholistic assumptions held to by gestalt therapy need not be tortured too extensively in order to become more in line with the metaphysics of Zen, which personally I have concluded have great utilitarian as well as spiritual implications.

PSYCHOTHERAPY: MODELS FOR GROWTH

Eric H. Marcus, M.D.

I long ago discovered that I could avoid much frustration as a therapist if, in the initial stages of contact with a client, I could recognize his basic contractual position. What did he want from me as a therapist? I have developed the following simple model for viewing the new client, the use of which has saved me considerable frustration.

Imagine a spectrum divided into three portions. The left third I designate the custodial range, the middle third the medical range, and the right third the growth range. The custodial range includes people primarily interested in maintaining the status quo. They just don't want to feel any worse! Obviously, attempting to change them is a frustrating and probably futile task.

The middle third, the medical range, includes people seeking help in order to feel better. They want relief from psychological "ailments." They seek doctors, counselors, help givers, hoping that if they cooperate and follow directions, they will eventually get what they want—to feel better.

The right third of the spectrum, the growth range, refers to people seeking to increase their human potential. These people go to "growth centers" such as Esalen, engage in a wide variety of humanistic therapy experiences, get involved in various spiritual disciplines. Of course there is an overlap between the medical and growth ranges; many of the techniques of the growth movements are applicable to those within the medical range.

Recently I also began viewing new clients from an Eastern frame of reference rather than the conventional psychiatric nosology.* Our psychiatric diagnostic system involves only psychopathology; there is no description of normal (or supranormal) states. The "classification" system that I find most useful is the chakra concept.

Chakras are centers of energy as described in Hindu Yoga philosophy. Interestingly, similar centers are mentioned in ancient Hebrew literature. Each energy center is associated with a specific color, energy vibration, physical and psychological functionings.

The first chakra, located at the base of the spine, has as its function existence and survival. It is referred to as the root chakra. Grounding is a function of this chakra. Persons existing primarily at the first chakra are characterized by a "holding on" orientation. These people would fit within the custodial range of the previously described spectrum.

The second chakra, located deep within the pelvis, has to do with procreation and sexual functioning. A great interest in sexuality is frequently observed in persons who have moved from the first to the second chakra.

The third chakra, located at the solar plexus, is the seat of mastery of the environment, strivings, accomplishments, educational and vocational achievements, the so-called ego functions. Emotionality (anger, grief, frustration, etc.) are also third-chakra functions. Conditional love, such as between mates and family members, is a high third-chakra function. This chakra involves dichotomies such as love-hate, good-bad, success-failure.

The fourth chakra, called the heart chakra, is located in the center of the chest. From the dualities of the third chakra one now experiences the merger and union of opposites. There is now a very different perspective about one's existence as one experiences unity and unconditional love. The attachments which

---

*I am very grateful to Jack Rosenberg, Ph.D., for my first exposure to the following material.

caused pain (and also pleasure) are given up. Transcendental and precognitive experiences are frequently experienced by those with open fourth chakras.

The fifth chakra, located at the throat, has to do with creativity and intuition. Another function is purification, meaning the finishing of any unfinished business at the lower chakras. Being open in this chakra is characterized by acceptance of the world as it is, i.e., the realization that whatever experiences are presented constitute opportunities for growth.

The sixth chakra, called the third eye, is located at the center of the forehead. Its major function is knowledge, meaning a complete and total understanding of all processes at their most subtle level. This involves psychic as well as psychological awareness and includes a nonjudgmental witnessing of oneself and one's environment.

The seventh chakra, called the crown chakra, is located at the top of the head. Functioning at this level has been variously described as the state of Nirvana, Zen, Samadhi, etc. It represents the state of cosmic consciousness.

Practically all Western psychotherapies deal only with second and third-chakra issues. For example, Freudian psychoanalysis and Reichian therapy are second-chakra (sexual energy) theoretical systems. Adlerian psychology, gestalt therapy, and transactional analysis could be considered as third-chakra therapies. The only Western psychotherapies I consider to be fourth-chakra therapies are Jungian analysis and psychosynthesis. The fourth chakra is the transition to the higher or spiritual chakras. Persons frequently experience severe despair as they move between the third and fourth chakra. This could be called "existential aloneness"—an awareness of one's own mortality and ultimate death. This is not the depression one encounters at lower chakras, which is due to neurotic processes.

A goal, if one is interested in the full range of human potential, is having access to the energies at all the chakra levels. Unfortunately, most of us are "stuck" at certain chakras. For example, persons with extensive hallucinogenic drug experiences may be

Scott

functioning at the sixth and seventh chakras while having absolutely no grounding at the lower chakras. Therapy would involve considerable attention to the first three chakras. On the other hand, persons who have already made considerable growth strides at the lower chakras may be ready for experiences at the fourth and higher levels. By means of Neo-Reichian breathing techniques, imagery, and Eastern practices such as meditation or mantras, a person may be guided toward the higher chakras.

Eastern practices are valuable adjuncts to psychotherapy regardless of the chakra level. For example meditation, in its many forms, is useful both as an exploratory and integrative method. One common purpose of all meditation techniques is to stop your "computer." Access to higher consciousness can only happen if you (temporarily) stop thinking. Our computers are constantly going, and meditation is a way of jamming them. On the lower levels, certain basic functions improve, e.g., blood pressure drops, tension drops; while on higher levels, new states of consciousness become accessible.

An optimal approach to growth is one which helps a person achieve *flexibility*, i.e., functioning at different levels, different chakras. For example, someone may function predominantly at the upper spiritual chakras without grounding at the lower levels. But lower-level grounding is a necessity for those who live in an urban Western culture. Conversely, when a client is reasonably well finished with his "hangups" he may wish to experience higher states of consciousness. There are techniques available to facilitate access to those chakras, such as meditations and breathing methods.

A comprehensive growth model includes five components. The first is *therapy*—of the type best suited to the needs of the client. Most clients can benefit from a body therapy experience, such as Rolfing, Reichian, bioenergetics, or an Eastern system such as Aikido. Another of the alternative types of therapy that the client can choose from are what I call cognitive therapies, such as psychoanalysis, rational-emotive therapy, transactional analysis. There are also therapies that deal extensively with emotions, such as primal therapy and the various body therapies. Certain other therapies such as psychosynthesis work primarily with imagery, a powerful symbolic way of influencing a person's life pattern.

The second component to be considered is *nutrition*. The effect of diet is quite remarkable on the mind and body, and much energy in counseling can be wasted with someone whose diet consists of coffee, coke, and chocolate fudge cake. At a more subtle level, there are diagnostic tests available by which a hair sample is analyzed to determine mineral deficits. Not infrequently, changing the body chemistry significantly "cures" a psychological problem.

diet

The third vital component, previously mentioned, is *meditation*. Meditation can take anywhere from two to twenty minutes. Most important is that it be done regularly. There are active techniques, e.g., involving walking, as well as many which are to be done sitting.

The fourth component is *exercise*, which nowadays is undergoing a transition. Western sports are primarily competitive and stress muscle and endurance building; the body thereby becomes an object to be built up, as with any other skill. There is no integration of the mind and body—an athlete's or dancer's body remains only an instrument. Eastern philosophies consider the body-mind as a unit. Effective physical exercise techniques that take into account this body-mind level include Chinese Tai Chi, Hindu Yoga, and Japanese Aikido.

The fifth component, *keeping a journal*, is an effective way of integrating between therapy sessions. The best times to write are upon awakening or before falling asleep. Writing one's thoughts helps empty the mind of compulsive, repetitive word "clutter."

It is obviously impossible for one therapist to be skilled at all of the Eastern and Western approaches. But this overview of the complex scheme of "human potential" indicates the potential inadequacy of a narrowly trained psychotherapist.

My personal development has involved continuing exposure to a wide variety of approaches. I can thus serve as a resource person and direct my clients into appropriate endeavors complementing their psychotherapy.

NEW GROUP

Eric H. Marcus, M.D.

Much of gestalt therapy is done in a group format. These may consist of weekly sessions or weekend workshops. In conducting such groups, I have evolved a general method of proceeding with the early sessions, regardless of the type of group.

I first observe what people do as they come into the room. What do they look like? How do they greet me? How do they greet each other? Where do they sit? How uptight do they appear? How many sit on the floor? Do they hold notebooks? (If it is a professional workshop, they may be ready to "take notes.")

My first efforts are directed toward forming a *trusting* group, which may take anywhere from a half-hour to four months! My theory, my philosophy, is that effective gestalt work takes place more readily within a trusting group. Some gestalt therapists view their roles differently. Their position could be expressed as: "I'm available. You wanted me, you hired me. I'm here. What do you want from me? My obligation is to be here and be available. If you (group) decide to sit and be uptight for six months, then that's your choice." I take a more active role in helping the group to move.

I usually start with a series of rounds. (A round is having each person consecutively respond to my question or request.) In a new group, rounds are an excellent means of initial sharing and exposure. They help the participants to become acquainted and to develop trust in the situation and each other. One of the first rounds is to find out what expectations everyone has. Thus, fantasies are exposed. (Typical responses are, "I expect to be bored." "I expect to be entertained." "I expect to work.") Next, I want to know what they expect from me and how realistic their expectations are. Did they come for information? Did they come to watch other people work? Did they come for personal growth? By means of rounds they reveal and share these kinds of things. Another round might then be focused on the (immediate) environment. How do they feel about the environment? First the inanimate environment—it is less threatening. Then the animate environment—the people. They then start becoming aware that a group is being formed.

I encourage a certain amount of initial group interaction. For example, one person may say to another, "When you first walked in I didn't like you." At this point I won't get into gestalt work, preferring just to stay with initial impressions, ""I like you." "I don't like you." "You looked scared when I saw you in the elevator." Gradually a group atmosphere is built. If there is too much intellectualizing, I'll comment on it but nevertheless allow some. At first I don't want negative interactions; that may destroy group trust before it has a chance to develop. Much initial "negativity" later turns out to be transference. Persons remind each other of their ex-husbands, fathers, etc. I favor acknowledging these transferences and request that the encounter be postponed until later in the workshop (or subsequent session).

Some people are initially annoyed about the "lack of freedom" in gestalt, such as the "rules" and the vocabulary. There are several ways to introduce gestalt ground rules. I introduce them as they are violated in the rounds. Somebody will say, "I feel that you are . . ." And I say, "Please use the word *feeling* only for feelings and please use some other word if you are imagining. We all need to agree on what words mean." If someone talks *about* someone who is present, I ask them to speak directly to that person.

After the rounds I encourage a short period of free flow. Amazing material comes out, such as what happened on the elevator, who sat next to whom, or who didn't sit next to whom. Each person of course was behaving in his customary style, so the for work. For example, a person says to another member, "You just sat out there and you didn't say a word to anybody. And I resented the way you isolated yourself." And the reply is, "Well, yes, that's how I approach all new situations. That's my life-style." I now have a focus in working with that person.

The next step is to have the group do a series of pairing exercises—to meet each other on an individual level. I think that's extremely important. In workshops I've attended where I have not had the chance to meet people individually, even for five minutes, I've often felt distant from many persons. Perhaps I then made contact during a break. However, the break chitchat is not the same as these intensive five-minute encounters. I have them change partners after each exercise until they have met at least three-fourths of the group. One exercise is, "What I want you to know about me is . . .'" Other exercises are, "What have you suppressed?" "Tell me about your phoniness." Gradually I offer more intensive experiences, the nature of which depends on many circumstances. For example, I may have them do exercises involving an increasing degree of physical contact.

One important aspect in groups where people work (or learn) together is the issue of confidentiality. The topic may be introduced by discussion—for instance, whether or not the material in the group will get back to coworkers. Then the members get more specific and talk about whom they trust *within* the group—if they feel like sharing with that person or not. I doubt whether the issue of confidentiality is fully settled with this initial discussion. However, this early focus certainly lubricates interaction, and eventually a deeper level of trust will develop.

This method of starting work with a new group introduces the participants to the methodology and philosophy of gestalt in an active way. It is quite a different experience than if I were to talk *about* gestalt. As the sessions (or workshop) continue, it becomes progressively easier for the participants to become involved in the process.

The principles illustrated in this chapter can be repeatedly seen operating in the transcriptions of work sessions that appear throughout the book.

PRESENTING GESTALT TO LARGE GROUPS

Eric H. Marcus, M.D.

I am sometimes in the position of presenting gestalt to large groups, either professional or lay audiences, who are interested in hearing about gestalt—as distinguished from therapy or workshop groups. After numerous public lectures I became bored with the lecture format and began giving the entire audience gestalt experiences preceded and followed by "microlectures." This provides the audience with an experience similar to a workshop group, in that I offer everyone an opportunity to participate. This is consistent with gestalt philosophy, i.e., a total experience is more meaningful than an intellectual one. I always explicitly state that anyone wishing not to participate may decline.

The following are excerpts of an edited transcript of such a microlecture approach with a lay audience in Denver. It is typical of the way in which I now present gestalt to large groups.

. . . I am now going to give you some experiences in meaningful and nonmeaningful communication. I divide nonmeaningful communication into three types of "shit":

You are first going to experience "chicken shit." Find a partner and have a two-minute encounter, making every effort to say absolutely nothing of any significance! (Laughter) Avoid anything meaningful. (Pause)

The second type is called "bullshit." Bullshit sometimes is known as psychodynamics or interpretations, and now you get to play therapist and analyze each other. Pair up again and give each other explanations and theories about anything you can think of. (Pause)

The third type is called "elephant shit," which of course is the heaviest. Elephant shit includes lectures and discussions about gestalt therapy, politics, religion, and anything else of weighty nature. (Audience is asked to pair up again and experience elephant shitting.)

Meaningful communication is the use of "I-language." I-language involves revelations of the speaker's feelings as well as reactions to the person spoken with. Feelings include emotional states, psychosomatic manifestations, skin sensations, postural ones, etc. (Group is asked to pair up again and spend a few minutes speaking in I-language.)

I'm going to ask volunteers to come up and demonstrate some gestalt principles. What you're going to do is the most difficult experience, according to Fritz Perls. It's called being obvious. You are to look at each other and alternately comment to each other on what is obvious. Obvious means that the information must come to you by means of any of your senses. Anytime you say something that is not obvious, I'll point it out.

Male Volunteer to Partner: It's obvious to me that you have some giggly energy.

Marcus: That's diagnostic. You took some basic information and then you made some diagnostic assumptions about energy concepts. You don't know her "diagnosis." Just stay with the obvious.

Male: It's obvious to me that you're laughing, smiling about something.

Marcus: If you had stopped after you said "smiling," OK, but smiling *about something* is a speculation. She may be smiling about nothing! (To the girl volunteer) OK, your turn.

Female: You've got curly hair.

Male: It's obvious to me you have two earrings.

Female: It's obvious you have a beard.

Male: It's obvious you have a nose.

Marcus: You're both now using your eyes and you're reporting visual information.

Female: It's obvious you have a nice face.

Marcus: You made a value judgment. What you did was say something obvious and then make a judgment. There's nothing wrong with value judgments as long as you recognize that's what they are. If you confuse value judgments with what's obvious, then you can get into trouble, because other people will have different value judgments about the same information. Now combine the obvious with a speculation, clearly labeling each. For example, "It is obvious to me that you have wrinkles in your forehead, and I imagine that you are concentrating hard." You're acknowledging your imagination, and the other person can agree or disagree with your imagination.

Female: It's obvious you're blushing, I imagine you're embarrassed.

Male: It's obvious to me that you have earrings, I imagine you like your earrings."

Marcus: That's correct. She may not like earrings at all. She may be putting them on because she has a "guilt complex" and those are her mother's earrings! There are many reasons why she could be wearing them.

Group: Is this a way of facilitating communications?

Marcus: Yes, by first agreeing on a common language. Communication requires language. If one person is speculating and the other is not, and they don't recognize the difference because they don't have a common language, it really screws up communication.

Group: Is it possible that we can keep those ideas in mind but not use "it's obvious" and "I suspect?"

Marcus: Of course, as long as the other person knows what you are saying.

I would like two other people to demonstrate another concept of gestalt therapy. I'd like you to start sentences to each other with the words, "I have to."

Male: I have to earn a living.

Female: I have to start a new job next month.

Male: I have to meet a lot of rules.

Female: I have to resign from my present job to take my new job.

Male: I have to meet the expectations of others.

Female: I have to try to please my husband and my children.

Male: So do I. (Great laughter)

Male: I have to go to work sometimes when I don't want to.

Female: I have to cook when I get home tonight so I can be ready to teach in the morning.

Marcus: Go back over the same material except substitute the words, "I choose to."

Male: I choose to follow a lot of rules on the job that I don't like.

Marcus: You've made a basic choice to have that job. If you've made that choice, then there are some have tos that follow. The basic choice in that example has to do with having that particular job. There are practically no real have tos. A basic gestalt principle concerns responsibility. If you acknowledge that you've made *choices*, a lot of burden is lifted. For example, "I choose to take care of my sick father" means that the obligation of have to is off my shoulders and I've made a choice.

Male: I have to earn a living, I choose to earn a living.

Marcus: So which is it?

Male: It's a choice.

Marcus: Of course, lots of people choose not to.

Group: What about choose tos, have tos, and the fact of our deaths?

Marcus: That's one of the few decisions that's not our decision. You will die whenever you will die. The timing, you may have some control over. You can choose to stop smoking. You can choose to moderate your alcohol. You can choose your driving speed. You may believe that thus you will have more chance of living longer. Ultimately, though, you will have no choice. I recommend a book that has made a big impact on me. It is *Journey to Ixtlan*, by Carlos Castaneda. Don Juan suggests that you imagine death to be over your left shoulder. Not to scare you or threaten you, but to realize that at any moment your life may be over. What you choose to do until death taps you is your choice. You have no way of knowing when that tap is going to come. One rationale for avoiding doing things is to avoid our mortality. If I "forget" about death, then I'm "immortal."

One thing we do in gestalt is to provide an experience of being different, to see what it feels like. I would like you to be aware of where you are sitting. Where are you sitting in relation to me, to the room, to who is on your left and right? Are you comfortable where you are sitting? Did you choose that seat by preference? Or did there just happen to be an empty seat? It is important to realize that there are no rights and no wrongs. There are only facts. I'm not implying any judgments. If you feel judged, be aware that you are judging yourself. Don't put your projections onto me and assume that I am judging you. Now, please sit somewhere else. (Pause)

How did you feel when I suggested that you change seats? Relieved, annoyed, irritated? When you got up, how did you decide where to go? Did you look around for a friend? Did you decide on a particular spot? Did you just drift with the crowd? How did you feel? How do you feel where you are sitting now? You have new neighbors now, you are in a different location. I'm going to ask some of you to share your experience. I'm not going to analyze or judge you. (Audience shares)

Now, I would like you to pair off with someone. (Pause) With your partner, I'd like you to make a decision as to which one of you will be designated as "A" and which will be "B." (Pause) Now I'd like you to think about three issues and in a moment share your thoughts with your partner. How did you happen to pick that partner? How did the two of you decide who is A and who is

B? Was the way you chose your partner and the way you selected A or B typical of your life pattern? After you have thought about these things, discuss them with your partner. Do not analyze each other, don't ask "why" questions, don't give "because" answers.

I may spend the remainder of the time in exercises such as the above, or I may ask for six to ten volunteers and demonstrate gestalt work.

I vary my approach somewhat with certain "problem" audiences: the naive and the hostile. In the past I have erred by confusing the two. Somebody will have asked me a "stupid" question and I have thought they were asking me a loaded question. They were only very naive, and no subterfuge was intended.

With a naive audience I proceed slowly and don't attempt to cover a specific amount of material. I would rather cover a third of the material I've intended and be sure that the audience understands it. I rely on constant feedback to assess the material's digestability. I don't try for subtlety or use sarcasm; naive audiences don't appreciate either and will become antagonistic. My wise, Zen-like statements are likely to be met with blank stares. I assume that each question is legitimate and constitutes a bona fide request for information. Regardless of the allotted time, I stress the basics of existentialism and the principle of responsibility. If I can transmit an appreciation of the now and a realization of what responsibility means, I consider that I have accomplished a substantial amount. It is like planting a seed that will grow after I have gone.

When I work with a hostile audience I try to remain especially aware of myself—of whether I am becoming defensive. A sense of humor is helpful—not taking myself or my audience too seriously. I try to keep a fresh perspective, to realize the actual dynamics of the audience. I use proportionately more didactic material for naive groups and more experiential time for hostile intellectual groups. The intellectuals will use theoretical issues to debate with you. With the hostile intellectual group, I let the person who has worked respond directly to audience questions. I forbid any speculative-type feedback, thereby restricting the feedback only to observations and reactions. Once speculations start, I have increasing difficulty maintaining control over the material and time. Sometimes when I get attacked I keep my mouth shut and allow some group process to take place. If I am lucky, there will be some people who were not swept away with antigestalt sentiment and will contribute their personal reactions.

A main point I focus on with hostile audiences is my overall goal for the session. I try not to get too far afield. I don't have to resolve *all* conflicts and make everyone happy.

Whatever kind of audience I am working with, however, my basic goal is the involvement of each individual in an awareness process.

As with workshop and therapy groups, the principles demonstrated here can be seen extensively in the transcriptions of work tapes.

SEMANTICS

Eric H. Marcus, M.D.

Although gestalt therapists by no means focus exclusively on verbal communication, there is emphasis on semantics. I believe in the premise that the way I (and you) speak is a function of my (and your) personality and not a coincidence. Accordingly, if our personalities were to change, then undoubtedly our manner of speaking would also. Gestalt therapists utilize the converse of this principle, namely that speaking differently will inevitably influence and change personality. Consequently, I will outline certain semantic principles which are particularly focused upon in the early phase of gestalt therapy. Keep in mind, though, that much gestalt work involves attention to nonverbal behavior.

One semantic "rule" is the avoidance of "why-because" interchanges, which result in explanations, justifications, and interpretations. The result is the accumulation of numerous therapeutically useless explanations, the client merely collecting justifications for his behavior. Explanations (technically called interpretations) are a legacy from psychoanalysis.

The why-because style of psychoanalysis is more optimistic than the earlier fatalistic, neurological, and genetic "explanations." An obvious example of the explanation game is the alcoholic who says, "Doc, I'm here to find out why I drink, so that I'll stop." Even with twenty explanations for his drinking, he is still going to drink! Now he has the theories, but theories don't change behavior. In fact, not only won't his drinking cease, but now he has new information to justify it. His role now is to keep the therapist supplied with "data," and he will receive new explanations! In gestalt, instead of why-because games we prefer the words *how* and *what.* Thus, response to questions are descriptive, and descriptions are self-limiting, compared with explanations. If you ask someone, "How did you behave? What did you do?" the answer will be descriptive. A "why" question might have led to a whole realm of speculation.

Questions are frequently considered as phony. Most questions are really disguised statements. Statements that most frequently need disguising are negative, hostile ones. The negativity is avoided by couching it in the form of a question. This process occurs often in encounter groups and results in a barrage of hostile questions followed by defensive responses. A simple way of avoiding this is to have the questioner rephrase the question into a statement. The statement may be "I resent you;" the question was: "Why do you always do that to me?" Once the statement behind the question is expressed, the focus then is on the questioner, rather than the questionee, who then doesn't need to respond defensively.

Another significant speech pattern is the use of generalizations. Some of the most common generalizations are: it, one, we, you, they, society, parents, the world, adults. Generalizations are ways of avoiding responsibility. Dispensing with them by substituting the word *I* results in increased responsibility.

In gestalt therapy the word *can't* is taboo. Can'ts are really won'ts, and there is a crucial distinction between them. A can't statement implies impossibility, i.e., no responsibility; a won't statement implies *options* and therefore responsibility for choices. Responsibility is a fundamental concept in gestalt—responsibility for actions or lack of action. In gestalt, we utilize no theoretical construct which avoids responsibility, such as the "unconscious;" we only distinguish between *awareness* and *unawareness.*

If unawareness is a result of a rigid character armor, then a "won't" is really a "can't." Nevertheless, I prefer to err on the side of the "won'ts," since this is a more optimistic position from which to work.

Another issue in gestalt is direct versus indirect communication. In sessions clients are asked to speak directly *to* someone rather than *about* them. If the subject isn't present, then an empty chair is substituted. Direct communication is much more potent than talking about it.

The last semantic point is the use of interpretations. An interpretation is telling someone what you *imagine* is going on in them. Projection is attributing to someone else what is going on inside you. This can be easily verified the next time you tell someone else what is "wrong" with them; try it on for size! In gestalt we make it very clear when we *are* interpreting by saying, "I imagine that . . . ," or, "I have a hunch that . . . ." The client then realizes that what is being communicated is the therapist's fantasy, and the client then has the option of accepting or rejecting that fantasy.

To summarize, the semantics of gestalt establish a common language between clients and therapist. The fostering of responsibility via semantics frequently produces personality changes, per se. Of course, the therapist needs to be alert for the passive client who will conform to gestalt semantics without a bona fide shift in his outlook. Once a client has assimilated and integrated the semantics of responsibility, then more complex issues can be contended with.

QUESTIONS & ANSWERS

Eric H. Marcus, M.D.

Before going on to the work tapes, I want to cover some additional methodological and philosophical points in the form of exchanges between myself and students. During the past eight years I have been training medical students and supervising psychiatric residents. The interchanges between us have elicited material covering a very wide range of practical as well as theoretical issues. What follows is a distillation of discussions from numerous such sessions.

Q. When you do gestalt, do you do things on a theoretical or an experiential basis? If you didn't have a theoretical basis, how could you respond in an appropriate manner?

M. The theory in large part derives from the experience. Let's take a hypothetical situation: Someone says, "I want help." On an experiential level, I feel myself getting annoyed and irritated, not wanting to rush to the rescue. On a theoretical level, I speculate that the client is trying to enmesh me in his "helpless" games. So then my theory really comes out of my experience.

Q. If you don't have some theoretical standpoint on any given interaction with a client, you might fall into a trap of playing into a game?

M. I agree. There is a body of gestalt theory, it is not solely an existential encounter. What happens in a gestalt training group is that trainees are taught how to watch for game playing. What makes good gestalt work intuitively is the smooth flow, which is due to the process rather than following a theory. If I function from a theoretical point of view, you would not see a flow, you would see a stilted, academic, intellectual encounter.

Q. Isn't it true that gestalt therapy deals mainly with process?

M. Yes, the purpose of gestalt therapy is to teach people the process of *how* to help themselves, as well as an awareness of the process by which they hinder themselves. The therapist helps the client to help himself by whatever techniques he feels are appropriate.

Q. Gestalt therapy assumes that awareness is curative; please explain this point of view.

M. If you focus on the *how* and *what* of behavior, the client develops awareness. When he has awareness, then he is in a position to make choices. When I do demonstrations I have people divide up and start sentences to each other with the words, "I have to . . . ." "Have to" implies obligation. I then have them say exactly the same sentences starting with the words, "I choose to . . . ." Most people immediately feel the obligations lifted and a sense of lightness when they realize that some of the things they are doing are really choices, not obligations. I estimate that awareness is 50% of the "cure;" the rest involves exercise, practice, and experimentation.

Q. If gestalt therapy is not interested in explanations of human experience, then on what basis can changes in behavior be effected, in the absence of cognitive understanding?

M. Explanations are primarily justifications. There are different types of cognitive understanding; explanations are only one type. There are other uses for your head, such as developing awareness, recognizing choices, and creativity. Rather than explaining behavior, we design experiments so that a person makes the cognitive connections out of an experience rather than by intellect alone.

Q. Would the "gestalt" be my understanding *why* I'm doing whatever I'm doing or my knowing *what* it feels like to do that?

M. The gestalt is putting together *all* of the elements. The word *gestalt* means the total, the whole picture, the understanding, feelings, sensations, awarenesses, and so forth.

Q. What specific concerns do you have when introducing gestalt techniques to beginners?

M. With beginners, I need to pay close attention to the process rather than the content. Before using a gestalt technique, I ask for their consent explicitly. When using the "empty chair" technique, I prevent long speeches by asking for a change of place frequently. It is important to maintain momentum in the dialogue; one way to keep the dialogue alive is to limit one polarity to a single short sentence. Another way of precluding a dry interchange is to have the client state his emotional reactions with the content. Also, I get him to pay attention to his voice; I may ask him to role-play it. If his voice is flat and he is saying something angry, I may ask him to pretend to sound angry. I watch his gestures—are his hands dangling at his sides while he says he is angry? I may ask him to make a fist; as soon as an appropriate action takes place, feelings usually follow.

Q. If someone says he's angry and his voice is flat, why not believe the voice? Isn't it meddling to ask him to pretend to be angry or make a fist? Perhaps he isn't angry. Perhaps he is angry and controlling it. Wouldn't it be preferable to work on awareness of process?

M. A first step in becoming aware of his process is an awareness of the incongruence of his words with his voice. With defensive beginners, such an awareness is frequently not obtainable, and therefore I may want to extend his boundaries of acceptable behavior by suggesting an experiment; namely, pretending to sound angry. If, in fact, the client was aware of anger, then the "pretend" furnishes the catalyst for the expression of the anger. If, on the other hand, he really wasn't angry or the anger was rigidly repressed, then nothing has been lost except a few minutes of time.

Q. Is gestalt group work mostly of the hot-seat type?

M. There are several styles of gestalt group work; the best known is the individually focused one. Another style is the encouragement of group interaction out of which an individual focus develops. Another style is group interaction where group members participate as actively as the therapist, the therapist intervening only when a gestalt "rule" is broken or the group process goes astray.

Q. What are the indications for, and advantages of, individual versus group therapy?

M. If the client is distrustful of the therapist, there is no point in placing him in a group, since he will not function effectively if he doesn't have at least one significant person he can really trust.

Occasionally I see a client who is so talkative or boisterous that he would be continually disruptive in a group. Also, very paranoid people make poor group members.

One advantage of individual work is the sustained period of intense contact. Some clients need to experience the nuances of contact and withdrawal and in a group this issue may get lost amongst many others.

Body work, especially with beginners or resistant clients, is best done in individual sessions due to the slowness of the "charging" process, which is boring for other group members. Guided imagery work also may be slow and best suited for individual sessions.

There are several advantages in group therapy. First, there is the opportunity for dramatization as well as innumerable modes of experimentation. Another important consideration is group feedback; consensual feedback is especially effective with resistant clients. Group energy, group momentum, is a potent force that may take a client to a space they would never have gotten in touch with had they not been in a group. Their work may go much deeper, due to the group energy.

Another advantage is the stimulation of work foci arising out of both group interaction and the work of others. Group therapy dilutes the transference to the therapist with consequently less dependency attachment.

Q. What is the role of transference in gestalt therapy?

M. First I want to define what transference is. It is a psychoanalytic term that refers to irrational feelings and fantasies about the therapist.

Q. In psychoanalytic therapy, transference is the basis upon which therapy takes place. Isn't that antithetical to gestalt?

M. I think there is a substantial amount of transference at the beginning of therapy and that gradually transference diminishes as the person matures. When the client uses his own eyes and ears, the relationship with the therapist equalizes, becomes more realistic, and fewer fantasies and projections are involved. Transference has a therapeutic value at the beginning of therapy. It is a way of starting a trusting relationship. Clients may give me a lot of magical powers which help them trust me *as a therapist*—they don't yet know me *as a person.* The power they give me is sort of a gift. Eventually they take it back and transference diminishes and I become just me; I don't have any more magic, i.e., they don't need to *give* me any more magic powers. They can then get along without me when I go on vacations—they can stand on their own feet. So, transference is "good" and "bad." It is good in the beginning and bad if it never gets resolved.

Patrick

Q. Then what are your own considerations in revealing yourself to a client—or not revealing yourself?

M. There are advantages and disadvantages to having my clients know what is real about me. The primary advantage of *not* revealing myself is to encourage projections and transference. If I don't reveal my emotions the client will usually project one onto me. They will see my expressionless face and say, "I guess you're angry at me," or whatever. If I don't reveal any personal data they will invent my life history!

Therapy is such a complicated and artistic venture, and the rules taught in the traditional schools are quite simplistic. For example, self-revelation is "bad" because it contaminates transference. If you do A then you get result B; and if you don't do A then that is good or bad. In my opinion, no matter what I do there are going to be advantages *and* disadvantages. If I "allow" my clients to socialize, they may experience growth *and* problems.

The greatest advantage of being self-revealing is the establishment of trust. The client will then see me as human, and his resistance will decrease faster. Also, self-revelation models behavior that is new to most clients. In practice, when a client wants specific information about me I may say, "I'll answer you, but first I want to hear your fantasies." It has been my experience that I get transference reactions regardless of self-revelation even in social, nontherapeutic situations. One of my considerations is *when* to reveal, especially with new clients. The decision is a matter of intuition and experience rather than a recipe.

Q. Earlier you mentioned the benefits of group feedback to a client. Could you talk more about that?

M. I'll discuss feedback in three parts: when to give it, its advantages, and its pitfalls.

There are a number of options as to when to give feedback. It can be given during the process of the work, so that it really becomes a part of the work. It can be given immediately after the work, which is the most common time for feedback in gestalt groups. A third possibility is to delay giving feedback and let the person have some time to himself. For example, if someone is very emotional at the conclusion of his work, I allow time for him to be by himself. A fourth option is not to give feedback at all. Very defensive people are likely to immediately rebut the feedback. They probably don't hear it or else what they do hear is interpreted as an attack. My preference is to let their experience suffice.

The advantages of feedback include giving the client additional awarenesses beyond those obtained through the work. Also, the client develops a feeling of enhanced group spirit and trust, through identification with the group. Another element is the client's awareness of the impact made upon others. Most gestalt groups are not interactional, and feedback substitutes for much of that process.

A pitfall of feedback is when the client's work is extended rather than expanded. Expanding means expanding whatever awarenesses have already been gained; e.g., transposing the insights into usefulness in the "real" world. Extending the work during feedback risks diluting the work. Dilution occurs in unsophisticated beginning groups when the person who has just worked responds to questions. Questions lead into new areas and thus dilute the impact and integration of what has already been accomplished. There are two other pitfalls that occur mostly in beginning groups. The first is group members not owning their projections; thus what occurs is rampant irresponsibility. The second is judgments made implicitly rather than explicitly. "You" statements rather than "I" statements easily obscure the judgments.

Q. You speak of integrating and expanding work, so I gather you deal mainly with intact patients?

M. No, mainly I deal with intact *people.* If they're intact, then they're not patients. There's no such thing as an intact patient, by definition.

Q. Would you deal the same way with people who are having serious problems? What is the scope of your techniques?

M. Some of the techniques I use are applicable within the medical model. Gestalt techniques can be used with schizophrenics who are hallucinating. Some gestalt therapists work in a hospital or clinic setting, working with very sick people within the medical model.

Q. Would you see a friend of yours in therapy?

M. Yes. Many people who were my friends are now my clients and a lot of people who are my clients are now my friends.

Q. What is your opinion about dreams?

M. I am not convinced of the veracity of the gestalt theory of dreams; i.e., that dream material represents projected personality fragments. There are numerous other psychological and transpersonal theories of dreams as well as a variety of dreamwork methods. The process of gestalt dream work involves using the dream contents as a projective device. However, does it necessarily follow that the dream per se represented a projection? Operationally, the gestalt approach is effective regardless of whether or not the dream represented the *same* projections at the time of the dream.

I find that the value of dreams is related more to the present moment than to the time when the dream occurred. It is not necessary to accept gestalt dream theory in order to use gestalt techniques effectively.

Perls said that a dream represents the fulfillment of a wish or else reveals a missing element in a client's gestalt. One approach is to have the person continue and complete the dream. Another is to ask what is missing from the dream. Sometimes I ask about the scene before the dream, or I ask, "How would you rewrite the dream?" My goal is to find where the dreamer's excitement is. If there is more than one segment to the dream, I may say, "Write the script that connects the two segments." Jim Simkin likes to focus on the most vague, inconspicuous element, the item the person would be least likely to identify with.

Gestalt therapists don't make symbolic interpretations as do Jungians, since all projections are considered uniquely personal rather than archetypal.

Q. What exactly do you mean by *contact*?

M. The spectrum of contact extends from isolation, to withdrawal, to contact, to confluence.

Isolation is being withdrawn *and* investing energy in keeping apart from others. Withdrawal is being apart from others with no investment of energy—being with one's self. It is what the psychoanalysts equate with regression, which unfortunately has a negative connotation. Meditation is a form of withdrawal, an inner directedness, a way of centering.

Contact is *not* losing one's ego boundaries *and* being in touch with someone else's ego boundary. There is a meeting at the borders. Confluence is losing one's ego boundaries. The Polsters (   ) wrote about confluence mostly in the negative sense, and yet I think there are positive aspects; for example, merging in love/sex or with music, etc. Dependency is a manifestation of confluence: "I can't live without you." Some people are very ready to make physical contact, which may represent confluence without prior contact. I remember once in a workshop Fritz Perls came in as a guest and somebody rushed up to hug him. Perls stopped him and said, "I don't want to hug you, I want to look at you first, I want contact first. I don't want to be just swept into a hug."

People in a so-called neutral state are nowhere. They neither allow themselves to withdraw (and recoup their resources) nor do they make contact. What we do in gestalt is emphasize the polarity and say, "Close your eyes, go away, and when you are ready, come back and make contact."

In the therapy situation, confluence is a very subtle type of resistance. These clients will do what you want them to do or think the way you want them to think.

Problems with contact are also, of course, frequent. Is the client looking out the window, or lecturing you, or making announcements? With beginners I pay much attention to the nature of our contact. Many clients coming from analysts are used to telling stories and speaking *at* the therapist. If a client wants to withdraw, I facilitate by perhaps saying, "Close your eyes, go wherever you want to go, allow yourself to withdraw, then come back only when you are ready." If a new client isolates himself, then I might invite him to have contact with me. Sometimes my "humanitarianism" takes precedence over strict existential responsibility.

Q. I think of gestalt therapists as offering little support to a client. It sounds as if you are different.

M. I recently read an article in which the author divided therapists in general into "warmies" and "pushers." I would say this is also true of gestalt therapists, despite the "indifference" stance that naturally flows from gestalt philosophy. The warmies are warm, supportive therapists who accept wherever the client is at and always respect the client's limitations, never pushing beyond. The pushers are not accepting of the client's limitations and will push clients beyond their limits. They are not satisfied with where the client is at. The issue is not which type of therapist is best, but which style fits each therapist best. Certain clients will respond favorably with pushers who would *never* grow with a "warmie." With a "warmie" therapist, these clients would be accepted as they are indefinitely. Others, of course, would respond to being pushed. My own style is a mixture; sometimes I support and sometimes I push.

Q. Aren't you essentially defining directive and nondirective?

M. A therapist can be directive and not push and be very supportive. He could dispense ample chicken soup. I don't like to use the concepts of directive and nondirective. Consider the issues in terms of a physical analogy. If I set up a situation where two people pair up and the goal is for one person to get the other across the room, the person could coax or gently pull them across. Someone else would kick or drag them across. What is the "best" way to get the person across the room? By kicking? By coaxing? By which way will they *grow* more? Actually the best way is for the person *to learn to get across on his own.* The next best thing is to get the person across *somehow.* Once across, by whatever means, the person is in a new place and future crossings become easier. The "physical" schools of psychotherapy stress breaking character armor by whatever means are effective. A gentle psychological or physical approach could take twenty years! Once character armor has been softened, it becomes easier to proceed with the remainder of the work. A gestalt purist would say that the client didn't do it by himself. He didn't learn the *process* of what and how he did. I acknowledge the validity of that argument up to a point. But expecting a person with rigid character armor to change by means of increased self-awareness only, may take an unnecessarily long time. After a weakening of character armor, an awareness of the process ensures maintenance of the gains and further growth.

In a training group I recently worked with a trainee and went beyond her own support. I attempted to do some Neo-Reichian work, and the entire time she was very resistant—physically and psychologically. The work eventually focused on sex and the closer she got to the area of sex, the more resistant she became. I tried to push her and was unsuccessful. I couldn't push her beyond a certain point. Whatever suggestion I made, she half-heartedly attempted. Several of the trainees became very upset due to the physical manifestations of her resistance—bodily tremors and labored breathing. The client (trainee) at no point said she wanted to stop, so I kept going until I realized that I was at a dead end. The situation *was* controversial. The more "classical" gestalt therapists would consider that I went beyond her limits and would be critical of me. The bodily oriented therapists might say that I didn't go far enough! If I had "blasted" her through her resistance I might have shortened her therapy by years!

Q. Do people ever become psychotic when suddenly released from character armor?

M. Reichian and Neo-Reichian therapists do not have difficulty in that regard.

Q. What do you mean exactly when you say you went "beyond her own support?"

M. The support we are concerned with in gestalt work is self-support. But first we need to discuss contact. Contact requires that the individuals involved maintain their own ego boundaries intact, in contrast to confluence. "Contact" means that at any point each person can make his own choices. Contact, i.e., maintaining your own boundaries, is self-supportive. The experience of making contact (vs. confluence) reinforces self-support. An obvious example is a separating couple where one partner says, "I can't live without her (or him). If she (he) leaves, I'm going to commit suicide!" What they are saying is that they are so confluent, that if "half" of them is "ripped off," they will die! If they can be taught to make contact with the therapist and others, they can then become self-supportive.

In psychotherapy, how much support the therapist will *give* is determined by where along the growth spectrum the person is. I attempt to give as little support as will cause the client a moderate degree of discomfort. Too much discomfort will inhibit risk taking and too little will stunt growth. Frequently with certain types of support, clients will take huge risks and move dramatically along the growth spectrum. I can do this, for example, in Neo-Reichian work by giving background physical support—touching on the stomach, touching the feet, stroking, etc. Meanwhile, with attention to breathing, their character defenses loosen so that they will permit a major crack in their character armor. Another question is, if the client starts to cry, should the therapist comfort him? Comfort may prematurely terminate their emotional release. However, sometimes the client is on the verge of breaking through, and some comfort facilitates the process. My style is to encourage clients to take big (emotional) risks. The client has everything to gain and very little to lose. If they are willing to take big risks they may save considerable time in therapy. If not, they are no worse off than before.

Q. Is there a possibility that taking a large risk may result in overwhelming their ego? How can you avoid that?

M. If a solid foundation has been gradually established I am not concerned about that.

Q. How do you determine how much and when to support a client?

M. A general principle is to give as much support as is needed to keep the therapy moving. As the person grows, I start to withhold support. The more support withheld, the less transference. There may be flurries of negative transference at the lack of support, but I have to decide intuitively how much and when to withdraw.

Q. What do you really mean by support? You're there as a human being, as a caring person. Would you be more definitive in terms of withdrawal of support.

M. One very good example of withdrawal of support is the technique of silence. Silence is a withholding of support or direction, leaving the client on his own. The therapist's silence almost inevitably raises the anxiety level of the client, who then attempts to cope, either verbally or nonverbally. One coping device is to fantasize about the therapist. Silence gives the client the responsibility for deciding his own direction in the work.

The contraindications to silence include work with frightened beginners. The stress of silence may result in many of these clients terminating therapy after one or two sessions. Instead, these clients could benefit from basic information about gestalt ground rules. Silence is obviously not recommended with verbose clients. Clients who drift from topic to topic are best approached by some directiveness.

Q. What about the caring relationship that is supposed to exist in therapy?

M. A caring atmosphere doesn't imply support *at all times* regardless of context.

Q. How does gestalt deal with indecisive clients?

M. Many people suffer by considering decisions an either-or matter. This is a trap, and when they realize there *are* other options, relief comes. For example, a woman works on whether she likes man A or man B, and subsequently realizes that *neither* A nor B is really the one for her!

Some people *say* they want to work on making a decision, but they've *already* made the decision. What they really want is for the therapist to confirm what they have already decided.

One frequent reason to avoid making a decision is to avoid making the wrong decision. These people shop around, attempting to get a guarantee of making the "right" decision. What I do in this situation is point out that they have made the decision to stall. If they can accept their decision *not* to make a decision, then they can relax.

Sometimes if someone really insists on my making his decision, I'll do so by flipping a coin and thereby decide. Occasionally, I set up a tug-of-war using two people representing the two sides of the issue. Usually the client's body will decide which way to go.

Another approach is to do a future projection. "What do you see occurring a year from now?" Another way out of a dilemma is to change the perspective. Ask the question, "What difference would it really make?" and, "Can you see the broader picture?" The person may then realize that his decision is really not very important in a broader or different perspective.

Another subject related to this is the directed vs. the undirected focus, as differentiated from giving or not giving advice. By "directed focus" I refer to giving instructions or experiments to the client relatively consistently. I am usually undirected with resistant beginners or advanced clients. Frequently resistance is decreased by merely letting the clients do whatever they want; thus there really cannot be a struggle with me. A potential disadvantage of this approach is avoidance by dissociation; e.g., if they are very verbal and facile they can avoid *any* focus.

The directed focus, although effectively providing a focus, may be the therapist's, not the client's. However, with skill and intuition there need be no problem.

A directed focus counteracts the client's programming, which is his way of avoiding the unknown. An important element of my work is the surprise element. I can really surprise the client by a sudden, out-of-context suggestion. Don Juan called it tricking. I need to trick him so that he will not react automatically with his customary character defenses. Using gestalt psychology language, what I do is rapidly reverse the figure/ground; by focusing on their ground, a new figure emerges. With resistant beginners I don't do rapid figure/ground changes, rather gradually focusing on their ground as they increase their trust and risk taking.

For you as a therapist, I suggest you become aware of your own basic style—directed or undirected focusing—and that you experiment by doing the opposite of what you usually do, i.e., change your *own* figure/ground.

Q. Please discuss the concept of the impasse. As I understand it, it is when a person gives up his defenses and all of a sudden he is kind of in an existential void. How does the impasse concept fit into a gradual growth process?

M. The definition of an impasse is when one no longer uses environmental support and has not yet developed self-support. It is the period of transition that constitutes the impasse. Here is a specific example: A woman worked on being "smothered" by men. I set up a situation in group where two men were to smother her with kindness. She became very upset and kept asking me to help her out of the situation. She was still looking for environmental support (viz., me). Then she cried and whined. She then attempted to verbally manipulate her way out of the situation. Eventually she stood up and then ran over to the door, took a breath and said, "Now I can breathe." What she finally did was get *herself* out of this impasse by self-support, in this case, her legs, and leaving a very unpleasant situation. This, of course, was a mini-impasse, not a major one.

Q. In the course of therapy the client needs to face major impasses, I assume.

M. Yes, there are "mini" and "maxi" impasses. There are some major impasses where the person will become physically and psychologically immobile—frozen. All of the person's energy is directed inward—we call this *implosion*. Perls wrote that after the implosion comes the explosion. The energy of the explosion is the same as that locked in the implosion. At the beginning of therapy the impasses may be minor. For example, a new client asks where to sit. The therapist says nothing. The client is stuck. The environment (therapist) doesn't tell him what to do and he is not yet at the point where he can make up his own mind as to where to sit. Sooner or later he might say, "Well, if you don't tell me, I guess I'll sit down here." A mini-impasse has occurred. He has made a decision for himself. It appears superficial, but that is the beginning!

Q. It is my impression that there is one great impasse that must be gotten through. Is that an incorrect impression?

M. There is no one great impasse that if gotten through results in eternal bliss. One needs to go through many impasses as well as approach the same issues from different angles. For example, if someone has had a severe sexual trauma—such as a rape—the person will need to work on that event a number of times from different perspectives. They may also have to deal with other sexual experiences that have nothing to do with the rape before the area of sexuality becomes conflict-free. The more traumatic the situation was, the more times the person will have to focus on it from different angles.

Q. What about sexual intimacies with clients?

M. I will deal with this issue in terms of certain pros and cons. First, the pros: If you believe that you and your clients are equal as human beings, then you are both entitled to the same transactions as any two human beings. If problems arise, then they need to be dealt with just as any nonsexual problems that might occur. Another possible advantage is the potential therapeutic and/or educational value of the sexual experience. The client may rarely or never have had a previous nonthreatening, satisfying sexual experience.

Now the disadvantages! First of all, the therapist needs to consider the issues of transference, countertransference, dependency needs, "acting out." Of course these issues occur even without sex; however, with sex they become considerably more complex.

Another issue is privacy; if the client is in a group, he will probably censor during his work for fear of exposing the relationship.

Another disadvantage involves commitment, the client "falling in love" and wanting an ongoing commitment. Is the therapist willing to give as much affection and commitment as desired? What happens if the therapist is having sex with a number of clients and each wants more attention?

A final consideration is ethics and reputation. Not only are there general ethical considerations, there are laws forbidding sexual relations, with M.D.s and Ph.D.s. Personal reputation needs to be considered and may depend upon what type of client you want to attract. If your clientele comes from the medically oriented community, your reputation will be more severely affected by having sexual relations with clients than it would be if you draw from the more sexually liberated segment of the population.

Q. What do you mean by *maturity*?

M. Maturity involves the realization that all of a person's needs will *not* be met from any *one* source and that therefore one must have the flexibility to seek out multiple sources. Two very important areas concerning maturity are the vocational and the marital. Many people during or after therapy make a major vocational change. They have realized that their job did not meet their needs. Regarding a spouse, the client may come to realize that he will only get a certain amount of his needs met, depending upon the spouse's willingness and ability to give. Instead of expecting one person to fulfill 100% of his needs, he must accept the reality that a particular person may give him only 60% of these needs. Consequently he can do a number of things: 1) attempt to force the remaining 40% out of that individual and thus relegate himself to a life of frustration, 2) play the martyr and decide that 60% is better than nothing, i.e., take the 60% and forget about the remaining 40%, 3) take the 60% from one individual and the balance from other people. How much you and I get from life depends on whether we want to risk getting needs met in a variety of ways. Attempting to change a spouse is a frequent factor in marital conflicts. According to Perls, we don't marry *real* people, but instead marry our *ideal expectation*. Then trouble comes. We very quickly realize that our spouse is very different from our ideal expectation. We then attempt to change the real person! Considerable anger usually emerges when one of the pair resists the other's push toward becoming the ideal image. I may have the couple work with sentences such as: "I want you to be . . . ," "I demand you be . . . ," "I am disappointed that you are not . . . ," "My well-being depends on your changing." It is a tremendous relief to finally accept others as they are and give up trying to change them.

One style of working with couples is direct confrontation of their transactions. Another style is to focus individually, the "classic" gestalt model, while the partner observes.

The issues of contact, confluence, isolation, and withdrawal are germane in couples' work. I focus especially on the difference between contact and confluence. Many couples are confluent; one person's welfare is dependent upon the other.

Another conflictful issue for couples is withdrawal; unilateral withdrawal may be experienced as a threat and rejection. It is difficult to convince a mate that the other's (temporary) withdrawal is not automatically a personal rejection. By withdrawal I mean merely having one's own space for a period of time.

Q. Please discuss the issue of responsibility in gestalt therapy.

M. Responsibility involves boundaries between pe misinterpretation of the gestalt view of responsibility ... due to people modeling themselves after Perls's concept of responsibility (and which is also reflected in the way he led his life). For me, the basic issue is as follows: If I am responsible for me, and you are responsible for you, *then* how much energy do we invest in the relationship? An important consideration is the balance between responsibility for me and responsibility for the relationship. I cannot be responsible for me if I do not know where my boundaries are. The issue is contact versus confluence.

There is very little written on impact in the gestalt literature. Impact is the effect—the consequences of being you—on another person. No matter what you do or do not do, there will be consequences. If you do nothing, then the other person responds to your doing nothing! The complexity is in distinguishing how much responsibility to assume for one's impact. Am I responsible for getting you upset at my expressing my resentment, or is that your responsibility? There is also responsibility for the relationship. It is my responsibility as to how I impact you—I can express my resentment constructively and our relationship benefits from the exchange, or I can be destructive with my expression of resentment.

It seems to me that one critical issue is whether my impact is authentic or manipulative. If I am manipulative, then I design my course of action specifically to create a certain impact. I am not dismissing manipulation as a "no-no." I am suggesting that you know and choose between manipulation and authenticity. Nonawareness of one's impact is a manifestation of lack of responsibility. Impact through nonaware manipulation is destructive to a relationship.

Q. You spoke earlier of *getting.* Is there any place for the satisfaction of *giving?*

M. There are various ways and reasons for giving. There is giving for the joy of giving and there is giving in order to "invest," i.e., get back. There is giving in order to placate. There is giving out of duty, a sense of guilt. There are many kinds of giving. I assume you are referring to the first type mentioned. Knowing yourself, what you have, who you are, means being in a much better position to give in a meaningful way. An immature person is needy and hasn't developed self-support and therefore is not able to give much.

Q. Do you really believe in no "can'ts?"

M. If someone has rigid character armor, certain behaviors might be can'ts, not won'ts. To say that such a person won't, becomes an absurdity. Where should we draw the line? If somebody says, "I can't get up and make rounds!" Is that a can't or a won't? Maybe for some people it is a can't and for others it is a won't.

Q. Why are gestalt therapists so reluctant to answer a client's questions?

M. Perls said, "All answers are given, we only torture ourselves by making up questions!" Most of us know the answers already. We refuse to accept the responsibility for the answers. One way of avoiding responsibility is to find an "expert" and ask *him* the questions. Then what usually happens is that we don't take his advice anyway. Or people come to me and say, "Should I get a divorce, should I leave my husband—give me some advice! I'm paying you for some advice." I say, "Okay, I'll give you some advice. *Learn to make decisions.* That's the advice."

Q. How do you decide when to stop a piece of work with someone?

M. An article by Bob Goulding mentions some criteria for when to stop a work session. The first criterion is administrative: the session has been scheduled for a specific length of time. Some people will always try to protract the session and never want to end. A second criterion may be an arbitrary limit of twenty minutes of working time; if you can't get things really going in twenty minutes, forget it, it's not going to happen that session.

A good time to close the work is after the resolution of an impasse. This is a natural place to end; the person is integrating what he has done. Another time to stop is when a major impasse occurs. Stop and work again some other time. Perls said, "Work to the point of completion, not the point of exhaustion." Actually, I didn't like the length of time Fritz Perls often worked. I watched him work forty-five minutes to an hour with almost everybody, and the clients would have a series of awarenesses. I don't believe that people can fully integrate a number of consecutive awarenesses.

Jim Simkin pointed out a common problem with beginning therapists—greediness. Not being satisfied with what has been accomplished, trying to push for more and then dissipating the effects of the work.

Schutz wrote about perseverance. Perseverance is going a bit beyond where the person would like to stop. This is good for premature stoppers. On the other hand, with clients who always want to go further, I usually stop decisively.

In considering when to close, an analogy I find useful is that of a stage play. When would I drop the curtain? It doesn't always have to be at the end of the play, it could be just Act I. Maybe it is just Scene I of Act I. People start working at different places in their play; someone is almost at the end of their drama, e.g., saying goodbye to a person, while someone else is just starting.

My decision about when to stop is based upon whether or not the person has had significant awareness and also on his energy level. With a beginner I'll stop after a minor awareness, but I'll work further with an advanced person, because I believe they can handle more. Some beginners have much stage fright and I may stop after some miniwork so as to build their trust slowly.

There are ways to stop the work when the work isn't over and I want a bridge to future work. A person may be just getting into heavy work and I don't think the time is right, for any number of reasons. I might ask him to make rounds and say to each person, "What I still need to do is . . ." or, "Mother, I still have to work on my . . . with you." I may support them for what they have done: "You opened up today," or "This is the first time you've cried." People who have a strong top dog may try to negate their work by saying, "I didn't accomplish enough, (therefore) my work is useless."

All of these techniques are mentioned for consideration, rather than as recipes. The closure in each instance depends upon the unique aspects of that moment.

Q. So much seems to depend on the therapist's intuition. Wouldn't an inexperienced therapist have to rely more on techniques and less on intuition?

M. That is the initial tendency. An excellent way of training in gestalt, which brings out the humanistic quality, is to have trainees start with awareness of *their own* bodies and *their own* reactions. *Then,* specific techniques can be learned. I prefer this approach rather than starting the other way around, that is, teaching the trainee gestalt techniques and after he becomes a "technician," then teaching him how to become intuitive. By tuning in to one's own humanness, creativity is enhanced. The trainee will either invent his own techniques or incorporate others' techniques in a natural, organic way. Gestalt will not become a rigidified set of techniques if the foreground is experimentation. The creativity that emerges from the therapist, in his openness, without memorizing a technique or gimmick, insures that gestalt therapy will not become a passing fad. Gestalt therapists differ radically. Polster, Simkin, and Laura Perls are very different, yet still remain within a solid gestalt framework. Laura Perls, for example, works predominantly with the body; she has a dance, body-motion background. Erving Polster works very intuitively, sometimes appearing surrealistic. Simkin is methodical, working with minute indications of character such as voice intonation and subtle gestures. Someone unsophisticated in gestalt would think that each of these therapists is doing different therapies. However, each of them is attracted to a different foreground. Each (gestalt) therapist is a unique person, so they *do* different things.

Q. Do you think that some of the things they don't do are because of a "deficiency"—not using a particular technique because they are deficient?

M. That gets into value judgments. How "perfect" can a therapist be? No one can do everything. Consider Laura Perls, who is fantastic with the body, but I'm certain "deficient" in other areas. Do we consider her deficient, or do we acknowledge her to be an expert in a certain style? Perhaps someone else may have moderate expertise in a number of areas, but not really be brilliant in any one. How do we label or judge him?

Q. What do you mean by *integration*?

M. I define integration as the process of connecting awareness with one's reality, which includes the translation of awareness into action. For discussion purposes only, I divide this topic into two parts: body and mind. Integration within the body occurs from body-oriented approaches such as Reichian work and postural work, as well as gestalt work. In my opinion, gestalt work is the least powerful of the body techniques. What happens with body work in terms of integration is very difficult for clients to report verbally. They frequently say, "Something happened, I don't know what, but I feel different. I have had a number of insights and connections to past events." Integration can occur during the body work or in the subsequent weeks. Usually the most dramatic changes occur as a result of Rolfing, people reporting tremendous changes in their emotional as well as physical state. Striking physical changes occur, such as shoe size changes, chest size changes, or a pot belly disappears.

I agree with the Reichian view that integration must include somatic changes. *Organismic self-regulation* means being in tune with inner processes and with the environment. If you are hungry but your mind is off on a trip and doesn't connect with your body, you are unintegrated and your body doesn't get what it needs. If you have unfinished business you can't fully perceive your environment, and behavioral options are thereby limited. Sometimes integration takes place on a deep bodily level; those who have had Reichian work have experienced integration without necessarily a cognitive component.

Integration may occur consciously (cognitive) or unconsciously. I have already mentioned unconscious integration as a result of body work. Unconscious changes also occur with verbal therapies;

frequently a client has worked on area A and they come in next time saying: "Things have really changed in area B," but we never worked on area B!

A well-debated issue is whether cognitive insights have the major impact for change or whether emotional release is primary. Which is the best and most efficient way to conduct the therapy? Transactional analysis, rational-emotive therapy, reality therapy, and psychoanalysis are heavily cognitive; the body therapies are predominantly emotional.

I have learned from experience and the literature that change occurs as a consequence of attention. Attention is fostered by excitement. Excitement can come about in a number of different ways: motivation, psychological drives, drama, identification, etc. Some people derive excitement from cognitive processes such as occur in transactional analysis. The client first needs to pay attention, and excitement frequently provides that attention.

Integration can be considered as occurring within three time periods: during the work, immediately after the work, and days, weeks, months, or years later. The work may, per se, involve integration as a process. At other times integration is the concluding element of the work. For example, the client may make rounds with an integrating sentence. A valuable component of integration is group feedback, which can point out holes in their work as well as help them make connections.

A valuable means of augmenting integration is by suggesting homework. I frequently suggest some ways to utilize or practice whatever the client has just discovered.

Do not be discouraged if someone does a major bit of work in a specific area and they are not "cured." The deeper the issue is, the more times the client will need to work on it from a number of different points of view. Sometimes I (and the client) am lucky in that he never has to work on a particular symptom or problem again. If he is working on unfinished business with a parent, he is going to work on that parent perhaps a dozen times; each time there will be qualitative changes in his work, little movements, not holding on as long to the anger, getting deeper into grief, or moving from grief into saying goodbye.

Q. What about feelings of sadness or pain?

M. Sadness can be either expressed or unexpressed, which is sometimes referred to as "masked." By paying attention to the "psychosomatic" symptoms, I may begin to suspect that a person needs to cry, but isn't. The symptoms may be a way of holding in and concealing the sadness. For example, if somebody feels tightness in his stomach, I may have him lie down and do deep breathing, while I massage his stomach; suddenly crying emerges.

Sadness may be masked by a different emotion, for example, anger. The person needs to experience *whatever* he is in touch with before contacting the sadness underneath.

Sometimes I suspect sadness when looking into a person's eyes. He may have a big smile yet his eyes look very sad. His voice may sound sad while the content may not be sad at all. Some people seem brave, "rough and tough," with a lot of smiling and laughing; I suspect that they are masking a lot of sadness.

Another avoidance is "spacing out." Sometimes the quickest way to reach the sadness is to say, "I'd like you to look at me." They may just melt, right there on the spot. Sometimes, though I suspect sadness, what emerges is anger. Since I don't have a "program" for them, I deal with whatever emerges.

If someone is crying, is he expressing or is he avoiding? All crying isn't expression. Sometimes crying is avoidance—avoiding contact, avoiding anger, avoiding loneliness. A client recently said, "I don't even feel in touch with my sadness, I just cry and the tears come out and I don't even feel connected with it." For that person "expressing" the sadness is of no value. I don't make assumptions based on one experience, but if every time, no matter what the context is, the person gets into crying, then I suspect that there's something else going on.

I listen to the various types of crying people do. Sometimes I tune in by closing my eyes or looking away. Is the sound like a child whining? Does it sound pathetic? Does it sound like grief, an open sobbing? Does it sound held back and squeezed in the throat? Observe whether the body posture moves toward more openness and expression or toward contraction.

Sometimes anger will follow after crying, and therefore I watch for signs of emerging anger. The first sign is usually making a fist, whereupon I prepare for its safe expression.

Whether to support (touch) the client at the onset of sadness is a matter of judgment. Will support abort or facilitate emotional release? If somebody is barely holding on, a gentle touch will allow them to melt. Sometimes I've seen the deepest release take place after the work is supposedly over. I may have said, "What do you want?" They say, "Well, I'd like a hug." They get a hug and it is like pulling out the stopper! But I never risk the possibility of prematurely terminating grief work by giving tactile support during the work; I wait until the person is really finished.

Another consideration is whether or not the sadness has a content. My priorities are: first, emotion with content; second, emotion without content; and third, content without emotion. I look for patterns; if someone always gets upset without a content, then I get suspicious. If the content doesn't seem to warrant that much emotion, then I need to explore the situation.

When a client begins to experience emotions, I consider three ways of proceeding. One direction is toward intensification of the emotion by a variety of methods, gestalt or Reichian. Another direction is to alleviate the emotion, by support or other techniques. A third approach is to allow the person to feel without attempting either to accentuate or decrease the amount of emotion. When do I do which of the above? If the emotion is distinctly reality-based, I merely am present and let them experience whatever degree of emotion exists at that moment. Their feeling is fresh, and this is not the time to superimpose childhood emotions or otherwise increase the amount of their stress.

I distinguish between grief and depression. Many situations result in a grief reaction, for example, breaking up with a lover or losing a job. If grieving is all that needs to be done, then I do no more than facilitate its natural expression. If I suspect depression, then I explore whether anger or resentment needs expression.

Q. Please explain how this differs from the Eastern approach of transcending emotions rather than expressing them.

M. The Western (psychological) approach to emotions is to foster expression. The Eastern (philosophical) view favors containment and transcendence. In the Western approach, emotional expression results in energy being discharged, thus leaving the person in a calm state. An advantage of facilitating emotional release is to develop the client's capacity for choice as to whether or not to express an emotion. Emotional expression affects interpersonal relations, since it influences the repertoire of transactions available between persons.

Emotional expression involves the completion of unfinished business, following which a broader range of behavior becomes possible. Bear in mind that the purpose of emotional expression *is* emotional expression, not to manipulate others.

A disadvantage of encouraging emotional release is that some clients get addicted to the process. Primal therapy clients sometimes regard their pain as a way of life. Also, emotional release can be avoidance of deeper feelings, as I mentioned. Consistently discharging emotions does not allow an opportunity for awareness of process; the client merely feels better and learns nothing about the possibilities of altering future behavior. I do not facilitate emotional expression with borderline ego personalities, hysterical characters, or immature manipulative persons.

Regarding Eastern views, I will mention only Hinduism and Buddhism. Hinduism fosters detachment from emotions and a type of denial, the object being to develop the higher chakras.

The Buddhist way is to experience the emotion as a feeling, not as an emotion, the difference being that an emotion is a concept rather than a bodily sensation. For example, "I am angry." Anger is a concept. What am I really feeling? I am feeling sweaty, I am feeling my heart pounding, etc. The Buddhist way is to feel the feelings, the sensations, not to label them as emotions. They urge intensification of the feelings. Staying with such an intense state leads to transcendence of the energy into higher states of consciousness. I favor containment with people who are "advanced"—

that is, they know how to ground themselves, are in good contact, and can express emotions. They may now be ready for something else, namely transcendence.

Q. In the course of your work do you find it to be a common pattern, say within a month's time, to see a big change in a person? Where at the beginning of the month they were fairly deficient, and by the end of the month something happened and they became much more self-reliant?

M. That is rare, especially in once-a-week therapy. It is not rare in weekend workshops. A weekend workshop provides an opportunity to stay in touch with a group for an extended period of time as well as time to withdraw and then later work again. I find invariably that many people on a weekend have some major growth experience. However, unless there is subsequent reinforcement, a portion of the gain will disappear. Ongoing therapy provides the opportunity for reinforcement. Another advantage of a weekend session is that some reinforcement may take place right there.

Q. Do people spend years in your groups?

M. People stay from one month to three years. People are saying good-bye every week. A typical group reaction is, "Good-bye, you've sure accomplished a lot." Eric Berne wrote that quitting group therapy is considered cheating. It is an insult to the group that anyone quits! My groups have considerable turnover. People are not afraid to quit, they don't get any pressure from the group. Many people return for more therapy later on. They are not stuck in a dependent transference relationship. In many groups no matter what decision someone makes they get analyzed by the group until they change their mind—if it's a decision that the group doesn't like. Recently someone said, "I want to go around the world. I want to take off for a year." The group's response was, "Do your own thing. If you need to live, live!" In another type of group you might have heard, "You're acting out, you're escaping, you're copping out." Of course, some people obviously are leaving for the "wrong" reasons. Then someone may say, "I'm really sorry you're leaving. I really wish you'd stay." But no pressure.

Q. It seems somewhat cold and impersonal to me.

M. I don't agree with that. I see the relationships in the group as mature relationships rather than immature, passive, dependent relationships. Relationships gradually become meaningful adult-to-adult, rather than parent-child.

Q. Purely adult-to-adult relationships seem cold.

M. By adult-to-adult I don't mean that people don't get nurturing. There is a great amount of nurturing going on. However, it is by agreement, not by means of manipulation.

Q. How do you come to the end of formal therapy?

M. If you were taking clarinet lessons, when would you terminate?

Q. (Answer) When I had learned all I can from the teacher.

M. The same answer applies to your question.

Q. Oh, but the outlay of money doesn't seem commensurate . . . (Laughter)

M. How long do you want to pay for clarinet lessons? When you are not getting much for your money with that teacher, it is not worth spending the money for lessons anymore.

Q. Would you describe someone who has been in gestalt and has left and you feel satisfied about it.

M. I conceive of a client as being on some step on a large staircase. Let "absolute" maturity—or happiness—be represented by the top level, and "absolute" immaturity by the bottom. A client terminating therapy is on a step somewhat higher than where he started. Perhaps he only took two steps up and yet someone else went up fifty steps. So I cannot tell you what step would be the ideal point for any person to stop. Assuming someone climbed fifty steps, perhaps if they had stayed in therapy, they would have gone up seventy steps!

Q. What are some criteria for having progressed up the staircase?

M. Questions I ask myself are: How much environmental support are they able to let go of? How much self-support do they have? (Again, of course, it's relative to where they started.) How much transference is left? How many decisions have they made in a satisfactory way? What are their goals in life? Are they getting what they want? How many major hangups are left? How realistic is their relationship with their parents, with their spouse, with their job?

Q. How then does the Gestalt Institute of Los Angeles decide when somebody is ready to be certified as a gestalt therapist?

M. By means of a theoretical and practical examination. Is the candidate, first, a human being, as distinct from a technician? How sensitive is he to the "vibrations" of the client? Does he have enough awareness of himself and of the gestalt process so that he flows with the client? Therapists will, of course, have different foregrounds and that is fine, unless the candidate is missing an obvious foreground that constitutes a significant resistance. For example, is the candidate focusing on a dream because *he* has decided in advance to work on dreams? Does the candidate pay attention to group process or solely concern himself with one individual?

Q. Reichian and bioenergetic therapists have a very strong emphasis on character armor, and their work is to get rid of it by means of various exercises and breathing. How does gestalt deal with "character?"

M. Gestalt theory views character as "bad." Character is a fixed way of reacting regardless of the situation. Perls's example is someone deciding to drive always at fifty miles an hour, regardless of the situation. Having no character, in the driving analogy, would be to drive as fast as the situation dictates.

Q. Well, then, did Perls advocate characterless people?

M. Exactly. Character is rigidity. It is patterns, programs, that have nothing to do with the situation. A person's character may involve shyness and no matter what the situation, he is always shy. He does not change his way of being; he can't enjoy many situations because he always reacts the same way. He has to pay a certain social price for his sameness, his character. The Reichian view of character emphasizes the actual physical structure, and by changing (loosening) the physical structure, the character dissolves. By improving breathing and freeing muscular tension, character armor is dissolved. Physical changes lead to character changes and vice versa.

One criticism of gestalt, however, is that Perls had only a superficial appreciation of body armor. For example, a client may be getting nowhere in a piece of gestalt work. The gestalt therapist may hold him responsible for that and say he is blocking, bear-trapping, playing stupid, etc. The Reichian would consider the client so blocked by his character armor that asking the typical gestalt question, "What are you aware of?" would be a superficial and meaningless act. It would be like asking a blind man what he sees on the street! His blindness needs to be alleviated before the question becomes meaningful. The Reichians would work on his body, loosening his muscular armor. The gestaltists would work psychologically. Either approach would ultimately be effective. However, for me the issue is which approach is faster. As a therapist I do assume responsibility for using whichever technique is most effective. Why use psychoanalysis and take ten years, for example, when gestalt might accomplish the same thing in five? Or, why use "pure" gestalt when gestalt *and* some other approach might be even more effective?

I think it is a therapist's responsibility to be trained in a variety of approaches. I feel uncomfortable if I don't continuously explore new therapeutic theories and systems rather than doing the same thing for the rest of my professional life.

I will now proceed with the work tapes, beginning with a number of examples of "classical" gestalt therapy, then continuing with discussions and tapes of gestalt integrated with other techniques.

TRANSCRIPTS OF GESTALT SESSIONS

A DIFFICULT BEGINNER

This middle-aged client has had no prior gestalt experience. As is painfully evident, she has great difficulty with the basic ground rules.

W. (Speaking rapidly and with great eagerness) I wanted to finish a dream I had a week ago. The dream comes back to me now very vividly. (Pause) My standing here, the great big red flame being front.

M. Who are you talking to? (She has been staring off rather than looking at me.)

W. I don't know. And beyond that I see a space and then the flame . . .

M. I'd like to know who you're talking to before you go on. (I want some contact with her before she launches into her dream, which I suspect has been thought about at length. Does she really want something from me or is she merely looking for a stage upon which to perform her dream scenario?)

W. I'm talking to you now, so . . .

M. Were you aware that you weren't looking *at* me?

W. I don't understand what I'm supposed to do. (Pause) And I see that red flame, tall high red flame, and a space . . .

M. What are you doing now?

W. I want to understand this dream. I never had it before in my life until two weeks ago and now I can't get it off my mind.

M. I notice.

W. I want to work on what that dream must . . .

M. How do you want to work on it?

W. By talking about it.

M. That's my impression; your way of working on it is to talk *about* it.

W. How else do you work on it?

M. I didn't have any opportunity to find out, because you proceeded to talk *about* it immediately.

W. I'm sorry, I don't understand, I don't realize what I'm supposed to do.

M. What you *are* doing is trying to find the "right" thing to do.

W. Well, apparently what I'm doing is not gestalt. I see the red flame, that's the here and now. I see a space before it and a space beyond it. (She slides again into her dream without completing our encounter.)

M. I imagine you're very eager to get into it.

W. Yes. And I see somebody in a union suit, but no face, a head but no . . .

M. What I hear is you're continuing on the dream, talking *about* it.

W. That's not working on the dream, by talking about it?

M. No.

W. That's what you call "narration," is that it?

M. Right.

W. What the hell am I supposed to be doing then. I don't know. Am I supposed to say, "I'm the flame?"

M. Notice your concern with "supposed to," how often the words "supposed to" come up. (Her top dog is very prominent.)

W. I just don't know what I'm supposed to do.

M. I have a suggestion. See if you can work on giving up some of the "supposed tos."

W. I see the red flame. (She ignores my suggestion.)

M. What are you doing now?

W. Narrating what I see.

M. At this point I'm not interested in the dream.

W. Oh, all right.

M. What did that mean, the "Oh, all right?" I notice you moved back a bit. (Her words are incongruent with her actions, in that she suddenly jerks and moves backward in her chair.)

W. I keep thinking of how I'm not supposed to say "supposed to." But what am I supposed to do, if I don't narrate the dream, am I supposed to narrate my feelings? Is that it, not the dream, but my feelings? (My efforts to get her to give up supposed tos are less than successful!)

M. My impression of you is that of a good girl, who is trying desperately to do the right thing, to do everything you're "supposed to do." I also wonder what's behind your perpetual smile.

W. I don't know. Truthfully.

M. You said, "Truthfully," and I wonder if you've been untruthful. When someone says, "To tell you the truth," I usually say, "You mean up to this point you haven't?"

W. I get your point. That's a very perceptive remark about my being a good girl and trying to do what's right, that's the way I was raised. (Long pause) I don't get the connection with that and the flame.

M. I don't either. I haven't even thought about it yet. Are you aware of the way you're sitting?

W. That's not relaxed?

M. Did you hear what you said?

W. Yes.

M. What does that mean to you?

W. When you said be aware of the way I'm sitting, I took that as a criticism.

M. Right. You're not "supposed to" sit that way!

M. There's almost nothing in our transaction that you don't interpret as a criticism. You're very busy trying to please me and doing what you're supposed to and apologizing every time you imagine you've done the wrong thing.

W. How can you know me so well?

M. By listening and looking at you.

W. Is it so obvious to the people?

M. Yes (Long pause) Where are you right now?

W. Agreeing that you're absolutely right.

M. For me, those issues are much more important, much more basic, than getting into the dream at this time. If you get into therapy, you need to unlearn all your supposed tos, so that one day you won't have to be an adult "little girl," sitting there terrified of doing the wrong thing.

W. Yet you have to be aware of other people's feelings, right?

M. Who has to be?

W. I?

M. You're asking me. Do *you*?

W. I'm asking you, but I'm also making a statement. I feel that one must, one should.

M. "One" must, any "one" in particular?

W. No, just people you deal with.

M. People *who* deals with?

W. That I deal with.

M. Notice how you lecture? Talk about "one," "you;" I have a hard time getting an "I" out of you.

W. I feel that I should learn to be more aware of other people's feelings.

M. So, we're back to shoulds!

W. (Chuckling)

M. Are you aware of that?

W. Not until you mentioned it.

M. I haven't heard the word "want" yet. (Long pause)

W. You mean, I *want* to be aware of other people's . . . .

M. I haven't heard you say any wants, all I heard were shoulds. My guess is that you're so brainwashed into shoulds that wants don't even occur to you. That your life is one should after another.

W. I'm not denying it, I marvel at your perspicacity.

M. I don't take much credit. You're obvious.

W. Unfortunately, it's not obvious to me at all. It almost makes me cry. It's not enough for me to say "I want;" I have to justify what I want, I should be entitled.

She will need considerably more work in dislodging her exceedingly strong top dog/underdog stance. At this point in her therapy, working on content rather than process would be futile.

A ONE-WAY TRIP INTO SPACE

This session is with a man in his early twenties who has used LSD extensively. He has had very little previous psychotherapy. A meaningful therapeutic interaction is stymied due to the absence of contact, and much of the session deals with this.

W. I don't know, now I feel kind of like I'm on the stage kind of, everybody's expecting me to do something and there's the tape recorder there. It looks really kind of ominous to me. And uh I don't know, I think the problem that I have is that like as long as I can remember there's always been just me. It's like me and there's nobody else. Uh, I mean I talk to people and stuff like that, but usually it's always like, what can I do for you, you know, what do you need, and I don't know, nobody, it doesn't seem like anybody is ever like given me any kind of attention, and when they do, I feel that they're I don't know like uh they're pampering me and that I don't really need it, don't really deserve it. (I have not edited his opening comments so that you can appreciate his style of speech!)

M. How about right now? What's going on? (I attempt to cut through the rambling and focus on the now.)

W. I don't understand what you mean. (As is apparent, he does not have a meaningful concept of the now.)

M. Relative to what you said, be aware of the now, how do you feel, how does the group seem to you? (Unless I can bring him into the now, I have no baseline from which to do any sort of gestalt work.)

W. I think the group is really good only I don't really feel a part of it. It's just me and when I was younger it was easier to do things because I was a lot more extroverted and then I got into doing a lot of acid and I got off into these trips and nobody knew what I was talking about, I would say something and they would look at me like what are you talking about? So I got into this hermit trip and . . .

M. Is the group here now? (Testing reality contact, is *he* still here?)

W. Yes.

M. What are you doing? (His eyes are staring off to one side.)

W. I'm talking.

M. To whom?

W. Uh, myself. (As I suspected, he is not in contact with me or anyone and really is doing a monologue.)

M. That's what you look like. You sound like a monologue.

W. That's the way I work, I'm always watching myself. I always have this feeling.

M. Now, what are you doing?

W. I'm trying to explain myself.

M. To whom? (I want to know whether he is speaking to me or again to himself.)

W. To myself.

M. Right. You getting any messages yet? About your isolation? (I hope he has already developed an awareness of how he isolates himself, perhaps my hope is premature at this point.)

W. Yeah, it's like I don't like it, I can't . . think of anything to do, or anything to say. (My hope for insight was premature!)

M. I'll give you a hint about what to do. Make some contact.

W. Don't know how.

M. Use your eyes, that's my hint.

W. I'm really very sensitive about my eyes. Uh, when I was a kid I had this uh . . .

M. What are you doing?

W. Well I'm talking.

M. You sound like you're giving a case history. Not only that, but you don't look at anybody, including me. Therefore, you're again talking to yourself. (Long pause) What's happening now? What were you doing?

W. Staring at people?

M. Staring, or looking?

W. Staring.

M. I want you to look at me, but not stare at me. (Long pause) As you look at me, say whatever you want to say. Whatever occurs to you. (Long pause)

W. I like the way your face looks, like a wise, old man, like Socrates. You look as if you understand what's happening.

M. Do you feel contact with me at this point?

W. I still feel very isolated. I feel like I'm watching a movie.

M. Any ideas about how you could be less isolated from me? (Another attempt to see whether he has developed any awareness yet) (Long pause)

M. You look like you're really deep in thought. (He is attempting to answer me by "figuring it out.")

W. No, I can't think of anything.

M. Do you know *how*, right *now*, you're isolating yourself? (An attempt to have him become aware of the *process* of his isolation)

W. I think I have an idea, but I don't really know.

M. I'd like to hear your idea.

W. Well it's . . . (His eyes again do not look at me.)

M. I'd like you to stay in eye contact with me.

W. I really feel uh when I make contact with people I don't know, uh it really feels weird to me. It just doesn't feel natural. And uh I feel kind of like I'm putting on a show or something or other. The other person is putting on a show and there's this, I don't know, this sense of games. (His ambivalence regarding direct eye contact is finally revealed.)

M. Do you feel a game right now? With me? (Again I'm interested in the now rather than past history.)

W. I feel I'm playing a game.

M. What's the title of the game?

W. (Pause) "Space out" and that's the way I feel, really spacy.

M. What I'd like you to do is look at me and whenever you're out of contact indicate so, by closing your eyes. Whenever you want to withdraw, make your withdrawal obvious. When you're ready to make contact with me, open your eyes and make contact. Go back and forth, contact and withdrawal. You decide when to do each. (Using the principle of polarity, I want him to experience *fully* contact *and* withdrawal—explicitly, not implicitly.) (He looks at me uninterruptedly.) (Long pause) You're being in contact all this time, I'm assuming?

W. Yah.

M. All right, I'd like you now to close your eyes and "space out." You decide when you're ready to come back and make contact. (In order to reinforce the experience, i.e., to allow himself to break contact) (Pause) Since you're looking I'm assuming that you're in contact.

W. I just got this flash.

M. What I'd like you to do is *speak and look* at the same time. What you'll find is that if you don't look at me you'll start spacing out and you'll wind up talking to yourself again. (An attempt at reinforcement)

W. Well I just had this flash and I'm spacing out. (My comments may have interrupted his "flash.")

M. Close your eyes, its OK. (I reassure him and suggest he withdraw again.) (Pause)

W. I think I'm ashamed of myself. I think that I'm really . . .

M. I'm not at this point interested in hearing any bad things about you. Not that they're not important; I'd like to get to them later. Don't forget to close your eyes when you decide to leave. (Long pause) Tell me what's going on right now. (The issue of contact and withdrawal is so important that I do not want to lose focus by getting any new information.)

W. I'm just looking at you, I mean without thinking anything. (Finally, he is in contact without his brain "computer" thinking, formulating, and rehearsing.)

M. Would you say the same thing without the "just." (He discounts the significance of straight contact by using the word "just.")

W. I'm looking at you.

M. OK.

W. I mean there's no box. (Prior to beginning of this transcription, he mentioned that he always felt himself to be in a box.)

M. OK.

This first, seemingly primitive, gestalt experience forms the basis for future work. His many LSD trips have left him ungrounded. I-Thou contact will reestablish a baseline from which to deal with his other problems, some of which he has already alluded to, e.g., his poor self-esteem.

FROM INTELLECT TO EXPERIENCE

The following work is with an intellectual, introspective woman who is much more comfortable in narrating her history than in being aware of what she does in the present. The work illustrates the difference between content and process, content being the subject matter that concerns her, process being how she functions. Important features for her process are her intellectualizing and her avoidance of being in the now.

L. Today I felt really spaced out again, and I'm becoming more aware of how—I don't know how I space myself out, but I know that I don't see things the way they really are.

M. Are you doing any of that now?

L. I'm trying not to. (The word "trying" indicates that she is exerting effort rather than going with whatever happens.)

M. What I'd rather you do is *not* try not to. I'd rather you just let yourself go wherever you go, and tell us what's happening rather than forcing yourself into some pattern.

L. What's happening right now is that I'm so confused about the relationship I'm in. (She confuses herself by thinking, trying to "figure out" the situation.)

M. What's happening right now—right this instant?

L. Nothing.

M. What you did is you went like that . . . (A gesture) (I am focusing her attention on her immediate behavior.)

L. I'm doing it again.

M. What is IT you're doing right now?

L. I'm trying to get in touch with something.

M. You're trying instead of *letting*. (Long silence) Now where are you?

L. I was just thinking about what I was feeling this afternoon and not feeling it right now. (She is focusing upon the past.)

M. What *is* happening right now?

L. I want to get in touch with this shit. I just feel an explosion coming on. I'm tired of me the way I am, I'm tired of not facing (Crying) what's good for me.

M. What's happening right now?

L. (Crying) I'm becoming aware of my facing it.

M. What I'm trying to get you to do now is give me facts.

L. I know what's *happening* to my mind. I'm very aware of (Crying) how unhappy I am. And how unhappy I've been for a long, long time. (She again talks about her past.)

M. Are you willing to stay with the *now* and let yourself be unhappy?

L. Uh-huh. (Long silence)

M. What's going on right now?

L. I'm feeling that I'm unhappy, and I'm saying, "So what? Big deal, you're unhappy." (Crying) I feel apathetic towards myself.

M. You don't look apathetic right now. Your face doesn't look apathetic. (Her words and behavior are contradictory.) (Long silence) I want to focus on *contact* with you and give you a chance to experience "reality," i.e., the "now." (It has become apparent to me that she is so little in touch with what she *is* doing and feeling *in the now* that working on the *content* (her problems) would be futile at this time. Accordingly, I devise an experiment for her to become more in touch with the "now.")

L. My view of reality is probably different from a lot of other people's.

M. Are you interested in doing an experiment . . .

L. Yeah.

M. I'd like you to make rounds and look at each person and start a sentence with, "It is obvious to me that . . ." The only source of information for the obvious will be your senses, and whatever is obvious to you ought to be obvious to all of us.

L. Okay, I'm going to do it. (She then walks up to the first group member.) It's obvious to me that you feel concerned, Cathy.

M. What *sense* did you use to obtain that information?

L. Intellect.

M. That's not a sense.

L. I know. (Laughs)

M. I think Perls called this experiment one of the most difficult, because it's so simple.

L. I have a very difficult time with simple things.

M. Right. Intellect is not a sense. What are your senses?

L. Taste, smell, touch, hearing, sight . . .

M. Okay. So those are your tools. Start again.

L. (She faces another group member.) It is obvious to me that you have a hole in your pants because there is a patch on your knee.

M. The patch was the obvious, the hole was the explanation. That's unnecessary.

L. It is obvious to me that you have a patch on your pants.

M. You used your eyes—okay—go on.

L. It is obvious to me that you have a beard. (Laughs) (Long silence) It's obvious to me that you have a white T-shirt on.

M. Okay. As you continue now, I want you just to look at the person's face and continue the same experiment. (I suggest she look at faces because it is very easy to confuse observations and interpretations.)

L. It's obvious to me that you have beautiful curly red hair.

M. Are you aware of what you just did?

L. Yes. I made a judgment.

M. You made a value judgment instead of an observation. (Very frequently value judgments are made which a person mistakenly believes are obvservations.) Now I would like you to continue the round and combine your observations with your fantasy. (My goal is not to have her cancel or eliminate fantasies, but merely to recognize the difference between fantasies and observations.)

L. Okay. It is obvious to me that you are wearing glasses and I imagine that you're amazed.

L. It's obvious to me that you have blue eyes and I imagine you think I'm mixed up.

M. Any comments on your experience? (Long silence)

L. Just that I imagine things and believe that they are obvious.

With consistent attention to her process, she will increase her awareness of the distinction between the now and her various mental processes. She then will have a clearer option as to whether to live in reality or remain in her fantasies.

SMOKING

This work deals with the smoking habit. The technique described below can also be applied to overeating. The various elements of smoking are isolated so as to allow the client to focus awareness specifically upon whichever elements (of smoking) give him the most gratification. Unfinished business frequently emerges during this process.

R. I want to work on the cigarettes. Right now the only thing I've got to hang onto is literally those damn cigarettes! When I'm in a crowd and things are tight, I can pull one out and I've got a little nurturance. I can reach in my pocket and I've got my comforter. I carry my blanket around with me all the time.

M. They seem to have a lot of significance. Are you ready to do the experiment?

R. Okay.

M. Get your cigarettes. You will do your own inhaling. Otherwise everything else is done for you. We will explore and see where that takes us. Close your eyes. (To a woman in the room) "Light the cigarette for him and put the cigarette in his mouth." Take a deep drag. (Pause) I want you to say what your experience is. (This will be the procedure throughout. A person will hold the cigarette and give the client a drag whenever he wants it. He will then relate his experience after each drag.)

R. Someone gave me a nice feeling. I want that feeling again. (Inhales again) Oh, man, that was really peaceful. A gentle pair of fingers just brushes my lips—it's quiet—no one's disturbing me. Nobody's pulling, nobody's arguing, nobody's hassling. It's quiet.

Really a good feeling. (Laughs quietly) Let's try that one more time. (Laughs) (Inhales) Gentleness. Gee, all I've got to do is ask? Man I can ask you and no hassle! It's quiet, no hassle, no argument, no "becauses," no explanations, no guilt. I ask and it's here. Yeah! The only way to smoke! (Lots of laughter from other people) (Inhales again) Now I start to feel . . . an obligation. Nobody should be that kind. Nobody should give to me that much without a hassle. Pretty soon you're going to want something back. My cigarettes, they don't ask for anything back.

M. I think you're now getting in touch with something else. How about another drag? (A significant awareness has developed. The experiment is continued, to heighten the awareness.)

R. No. (Laughs)

M. What's happening?

R. Because, you know . . . hell, nobody, nobody, is so gentle, so quiet, so good to give that kind of good feeling and ask nothing in return. I don't want to ask anyone. I have my own cigarettes and I'll take them when I want them and they're not going to ask for anything back.

M. That's the key. Keep your eyes closed. Let's go beyond this point. I'd like you to take another puff.

R. It ain't gonna last. That's okay if it doesn't last. If I can get you through this only once or twice . . . that's enough. (Inhales) . . . It's getting hard to accept it. God, I'm so fucking used to people arguing with me. It's getting hard to accept your quiet, gentle giving. It's like I want to start pushing you away . . . before you drop all that shit on me.

M. Which undoubtedly brings back some old memories. (I suspect that unfinished business is involved.)

R. Yeah. They bring back memories mostly of dear wifey. Before I accept anything more from you—kind, gentle, quiet person that doesn't argue back— I gotta get one thing straight. The first drag was a different thing entirely. That first drag was what I was looking for in all those cigarettes. I'd like to have it from you again. I'd really like to have it from you without the argument . . .

M. You're gonna get it. Just say, "I want it," and open your mouth and it'll be there.

R. (Laughs) (Everyone in room laughs) I gotta get my guarantee, you know.

M. She's not going to say anything anyway. I'm going to instruct her not to say anything. All she's going to do is give you the cigarette when you want it.

R. I want it. (Long pause)

M. Would you now open your eyes and look at her? (I.e., the woman who has been holding his cigarette)

R. Thank you.

M. Are you willing to continue a bit longer? I don't mean necessarily with the cigarette . . . but continue working? (The work is not yet complete. I want him to bring his awareness from his unfinished business with his wife into the present so that new relationships can be formed.)

R. Sure.

M. I'd like you both to stay in eye contact and do whatever you feel like doing. I don't want to tell you what to do. I want you to let it come from within you. (Pause)

R. If you could . . . if you want to . . . give it to me without the hassle, without the argument . . . I'll try to accept it with a thank you and not feel angry or guilty or pulling the life from your gift. (Long silence) I'm aware of that mistrust again. I'm aware of believing you're gonna dump a lot of shit on me. You're gonna want a pound of flesh back. You're gonna want me to feel guilty and I'm gonna pull away. I'm just gonna crunch up; I don't need you. If you start giving with a price tag, well, I'd rather go with these. (Cigarettes) I don't expect you to break your back—just a little bit, once in awhile. I'm just gonna say "thank you." (Long pause)

As is apparent, he has used cigarettes as a substitute for meaningful interpersonal relationships. The present work involved getting in touch with feelings of sadness and hurt from his previous marriage. Hopefully the emotional connection he has made will allow him to again make meaningful contact rather than escaping into smoking.

SWEATY HANDS

This woman, in her early twenties, is a beginner in gestalt and this is her first work, which proceeds along "classical" gestalt lines.

M. What are you doing?

C. I'm looking at my hands.

M. You were doing more, you were doing something else.

C. They're all wet. I'm trying to wipe the sweat off.

M. I'd like you to say something to your sweat.

C. "Why are you getting wet like that all over? That's a dumb thing to do."

M. Be the sweat responding, so you have a dialogue.

C. "I'm scared"

M. Be yourself.

C. (To hands) "You need to realize that nobody's going to hurt you. If you would be smart enough to realize that, you wouldn't feel scared like this."

M. What does the sweat say?

C. "I can't help it, 'cause I just come out anyway. I don't want to. I hear that you tell me not to be scared, and no matter how hard you try, I'm going to be anyway."

M. Sounds defiant. Continue the dialogue.

C. "If I want to sweat, I'm going to sweat! It's the way I feel, I don't see why I have to cover up that I'm scared. (Getting louder) Why can't I just *be*? (Almost crying) Why can't I just be scared? Why do I have to pretend that I'm something, when I'm not?"

M. Good questions, got any answers?

C. "It's important that you don't look silly or stupid. It's important that you look like you're not scared. It's important that you look like you got it worked out and that you're not dumb."

M. What does "sweat" have to say to all that?

C. "If I can just be scared (Pause) then I feel better."

M. Say that again.

C. It's hard for me to be scared.

M. I imagine that what's hard is to allow yourself to feel scared. You're going to *feel* scared anyway.

C. That's right, I have a hard time accepting it, though.

Acknowledging what *is* constitutes one of the most important issues in gestalt therapy.

RETROFLECTED ANGER

This work illustrates the gestalt concept of "retroflection," i.e., anger and resentment felt toward a person are turned inward due to fear of rejection and retaliation.

L. My parents used to beat me, I used to feel sorry for them. (She starts to cry) I'm really pissed off at them. (Cries fully)

M. Do you see what you are doing?

L. (Crying) Yes! I'm mad at myself! Feeling guilty!

M. You're turning your resentment *in* rather than *out.* I have a suggestion, to really experience yourself being beaten. (A basic technique in gestalt is to have the client *fully* experience behavior in order to more consciously select options.)

L. You mean beat myself?

M. Yes, and if you feel like it, add some sounds or words . . . I'm sure there must be hundreds of bad things you could call yourself.

L. I'm just not feeling anything right now. (Sounds of hitting) I *do* hit myself sometimes, against the wall.

M. What's one of your favorite put-downs? What do you call yourself?

L. Weak.

M. Okay, beat yourself with that.

L. Weak! Weak! (Beating self) Weak, weak, weak, weak! (Pounds self many times—to tears)

M. What's happening now?

L. I'm thinking that I care more about other people than I do for myself (She has developed an important awareness.)

M. Say that again. (Important awarenesses are emphasized by having the client repeat the statements.)

L. I care more about others than I do for myself. I don't know what to do right now. (Crying) I don't know what to do with my feelings.

M. You're at an impasse. (She is now stuck—i.e., she has had enough of turning her hostility inward and is not yet at the realization of wanting to direct her hostility outward.) What are you feeling right now?

L. (Crying)

M. Okay, feel it. (Heavy crying) Let sounds out.

L. I feel that when I hit myself I want to hit OUT at everything. (She is now beyond the impasse.)

M. Finally. (Heavy crying)

L. I don't want to hit myself anymore.

M. What I'd like you to do now is go around and hit everybody and do unto them some of the oppressive things that you do unto yourself. (Now she will experience the other polarity, i.e., being the aggressor.)

L. You mean verbally?

M. You can add words if you feel like it but use words AND the bataca.*

L. (Approaches the first group member) This is for the way you're holding yourself down! (Crying and hitting)

L. (Moves to next person) This is for the way you don't do anything. (Hits) You just keep on hobbling around.

L. This is for the way you always give IN. ALWAYS give in. (Crying) (Hitting) This is for the way you flake. This is for the way you *quit.*

L. This is for your operation. (Crying) That's what I *hate.* (Crying heavily)

L. This is for your *stomach*! This is for your *gut*! This is for your GUT! (Hits very hard several times) (Screams)

---

*A bataca is a foam rubber club.

Her rage is being released. She is experiencing the reversal of a life-long pattern of turning aggression inward. She also will realize that in spite of her vehemence, there will be no retribution or rejection, and therefore she will develop increased self-confidence.

GESTALT AND "PSYCHOSOMATIC" SYMPTOMS

The gestalt precept that unfinished gestalts always press for completion is illustrated by this work. A young woman commences with a "psychosomatic" symptom and quickly elicits an emotionally powerful unfinished situation.

C. I give myself very intense anxiety attacks. I was aware last night I could feel tenseness in places of my body that I have previously felt tenseness. I'm wanting guidance . . .

M. I'd like to use the Neo-Reichian approach. (I anticipate strong emotions arising and therefore proceed with her lying down and doing some deep breathing.)

C. (Taking deep breaths)

M. Images may or may not come to you. Be aware if they do or if a memory of anything comes.

C. (Breathing deeply) I picture a house where I lived as a kid. I haven't lived there since I was six. I'm picturing my grandmother. I picture her face just floating through the house. (Breathing deeply) Flashes of other houses in our village. All sorts of people are just floating around . . .

M. Let them float around. You may or may not settle on any one person. (Allowing her to find her own focus)

C. (Long silence)

M. Be aware of your stomach at the same time. (The focus of her anxiety was her stomach.)

C. (Long silence) My grandmother keeps coming in and out. (Voice shaky)

M. Stay with your grandmother.

C. I picture her sitting up in her room.

M. Say that to her.

C. "I see you sitting up in your room." (Voice shaky) "You're sitting in your chair." (Crying) My grandfather died upstairs in this house. She's looking at him dead. (Crying) "I'm sitting at the bottom of the stairs looking up at you."

M. How old are you?

C. Oh, about eight. I feel very little. (Speaking to grandmother) "You look so sad. (Crying) You look angry, too. (Breathing deeply) You are kind of pleased and angry that my father's dad died. I can feel that hate in your face and you are just sitting there, (Crying) and I feel scared. It looks like there's three thousand stairs up to your room." (Crying)

M. Let yourself be scared. Breathe. (Breathing deeply will heighten the emotional charge.)

C. (Deep breathing) My mother's looking over at me and telling me to get away.

M. Anything you want to tell her?

C. I'm shaky everyplace. My legs are shaky.

M. You're a scared little girl. Tell someone about your scaredness.

C. (Crying heavily) "I'm so scared." (Crying) "What's going on here?"

M. Say that again. (Repeating a key statement will intensify the emotional charge.)

C. "What's going on? (Crying heavily) I don't want anything to happen to me! (Crying) Why is everything so scared around here? (Crying) Why are you all so angry? What did I do?" (Crying heavily) (She is now reliving the situation.)

M. Ask them again. "What did I do?" (She apparently has assumed some responsibility for the situation.)

C. "What did I do?"

M. Ask them louder.

C. "WHAT DID I DO" (Crying heavily) What are you doing to me?"

M. Have you shouted ever? (Thus far she has not expressed her anger and I encourage her to do so.)

C. "DON'T do anything to me? (Louder) Don't do anything to anybody else. Don't be so angry. (Crying) Why are you hating everybody? (Crying) My father's coming in." (Crying)

M. Do that again with your foot. (Her foot had moved in an abortive kicking gesture.)

C. (Crying) (She complies) "STOP HATING EVERYBODY! Please don't hate me. (Crying heavily) Why don't you love anybody? I didn't do anything. (Crying heavily) It hurts. I didn't do anything. You son of a bitch! (Voice is louder) (Crying) I thought you would do something to me. I can't do what I want to do." (Crying)

M. What do you want to do?

C. "I want you to leave me alone. (Crying) I want to be someplace else. I want to get out of this house! Everybody hates everybody! I HATE IT! (crying heavily) I'm scared here. You all hate each other. You might just hate me too."

M. By "magic" you are going to have a chance now to leave that house, and get a new set of parents. So, name a man and a woman here in this room who can be your ideal parents and take you out of that place. (In order to complete the unfinished gestalt, she needs to experience some positive closure. She can *now* get nurturing parenting and thereby no longer hold onto the pain of that situation.)

C. Jackie for a mother. Actually *you* came to the foreground for a father, but I wasn't sure if that is okay.

M. It's okay. (Playing ideal father) "I'm going to take you away from here. I'll just pick you up and take you away from this place." (The work ends with her ideal "mother" and "father" comforting her.)

*Critique By John Stevens:** I just disagree totally with the new nurturing parent. It is putting the responsibility on someone else and it is not staying with the bad situation until she deals with it fully.

Response by Marcus: An eight-year-old *cannot* get past such an impasse. The new nurturing ending finishes the situation for the helpless child. The issue is whether the (adult) individual will now be able to cope with a similar (process) situation. An unfinished situation at the child's level is best finished with a positive experience of nurturing. To finish and integrate this work would involve connecting to present situations in which the same process would trigger off the emotions of the original situation. This exploration is best done either as a homework assignment or at a follow-up session so as not to disturb the just-completed intense emotional experience.

A PAINFUL SESSION

This is the third session with a twenty-six-year-old woman who has had no prior psychotherapy. She is rigid, suspicious, and intellectualizing and has little trust in her relationship with me. She terminated therapy within a few weeks after this session.

G. I'm aware that I overintellectualize. It's the way I've always been, I think, think, think all the time.

M. What you're doing now is explaining, are you aware of that?

G. Do you want me to tell you how I feel?

M. Make a statement out of the question.

G. I would like to tell you how I feel.

M. Do you realize the difference? In the two ways of putting it?

G. Not asking permission.

M. The first is asking my permission to do what you want to do, and making *me* responsible for what you do. What are you feeling right now?

G. I'm feeling lightheaded, but can I tell you why? (She is fixed on explaining everything.)

M. A "but" cancels part of your statement.

G. OK, I'll make it a statement. I am taking antibiotics and they are making me feel lightheaded. (Another explanation)

M. So what? What does that explanation do for us?

G. Then you won't think it's an emotional thing, like a relationship, like I'm here because I'm nervous, lightheaded or something. (Revealing one of her fears)

M. So you've already got it all figured out and wrapped up.

G. I'm aware I do that, but I don't want to go totally the other way. Isn't there a happy medium, someplace?

M. You're so concerned about going the other way, that you have everything all sewn up. You're complaining about being the way you are, e.g., overintellectualizing, and then a minute later you cancel out the impact. (Later in the session) It's really hard for you to be right *now*. You're always 5, 10 minutes ahead, or in tomorrow.

G. The present, I think the present's important, but I think . . .

M. "But" cancels out the first part of your sentence.

G. The past is relevant.

M. I'm not denying that, I imagine you're justifying.

G. (Later) I was sad the other day after I left here, *real* sad, and I cried, but . . . . (A good start until the "but")

M. See what happens if you put "and" in, instead of "but."

G. I can't go on, because it isn't what I want to say. I wanted to tell you what happened after I left. (She is annoyed because I won't let her tell her story.)

M. You can tell me what happened. The "but" cancels out the first half of your sentence.

G. It's impossible for me to talk. Because everything that I'm going to say is going to be about what I think. (Annoyed and probably discouraged)

M. (Several minutes later) I can't tell what you're doing. Are you biting your lip?

G. I'm sort of sucking and biting both.

M. Do that and be aware what that feels like. (Hopefully I may get some projective information rather than her usual explanations.)

G. (Pause) It's probably sort of . . . . It's infantile, it's being a baby, it's oral.

M. It sounds like you're coming up with answers to a psychoanalytic quiz. You're slapping labels on yourself. (Her top dog is very critical and immobilizes herself with judgments.)

G. What did you ask me to do?

M. Just tell me what it feels like.

G. It feels like sucking, the inside of my tongue. Feels a habit, that's not a feeling.

M. That's an explanation, a "diagnosis." Saying it's a habit doesn't add any clarification, because I already know that. Everything you do *is* the way you are. I take that for granted. I also take for granted that everything you do has reasons. Everything I do has reasons. I don't need to hear all your reasons. I'm hoping you don't take all my comments as put-downs. (Attempting to reassure her although probably not very successfully) The first step of therapy is having you become aware of the way you *are*. There's no point working on deeper levels if most of your statements are explanations and justifications. You need to constantly justify yourself to me. When you get beyond that, when we can be friends, then we can move deeper. If you trusted me you wouldn't have to keep explaining.

G. I trust you. I do, I'm like that with everybody. (Her attempt at reassuring me by means of an explanation)

M. I imagine you trust me to a certain point. I imagine that you trust me as an authority figure.

G. Well, yes.

M. To me that is a very superficial level of trust. You trust me like an "expert." That's not human-to-human trust. That's a trust for authority. (Later in the session) Have a dialogue between your teeth and your lip. Teeth, what do you say to lips?

G. Teeth is saying to lower lip: "I am pressing down on you, I am holding you down."

M. Say that again.

G. "I am holding you down."

M. And what does the lip say back to the teeth?

G. "It's a good thing I've got you controlling me otherwise I don't know what would happen." Just like the Perls films, fantastic!

M. Were you aware of the difference between what you just did and your previous interpretations?

G. Yes. Even though they mean the same thing to me. (Perhaps a glimmer of hope in regard to her persistence at explaining everything.)

M. Awareness by means of dialogues will make a connection with your guts. Interpretations are riddles that you solved in your head.

A painful session, a step-by-step confrontation. Perhaps a gentler, more accepting, free-flowing relationship with her would have held her in psychotherapy. Perhaps one day she will come back.

DREAM WORK—LIFE SCRIPT

This client's mother had committed suicide when she was a child. She presents a dream in which she is at a dance with her brother and parents, all of whom were blind. She has developed a life-style of being extraordinarily responsible for the well-being of her family.

M. I'd like you to close your eyes and see if you can get back into the dream as much as you can. In this rerun you're not going to wake up. You're going to continue to dream and write the next sequence. You're going to do whatever you want. So start with your eyes closed so that you can get into the mood.

B. It was a beautiful night, and it was fun to be dancing. And it was a nice feeling. And then . . . then I saw it wasn't beautiful. It was horrible.

M. It IS horrible. You're talking in the past. You're there *now.* (To intensify the experience it is important that she relate the dream in the present tense.)

B. And it's horrible! Dick! (Loudly) It's a horrible situation. I don't know what to say. There's too much unhappiness in our family. I can't say anything . . .

M. Continue the dream. There you are with three blind people. (Her dream ended at the point where she is dancing with each of the three blind people. I ask her to continue the dream, hopefully to complete a gestalt.)

B. Okay. "C'mon Dick. C'mon Daddy. Daddy, please hold Mommy. I'll have to lead you. Now be nice to her. Dick. He's scared. Please be nice to Dick. Please, Daddy, okay? Be nice."

M. Tell them what you're going to be doing.

B. "I'm going to help you all . . . I don't care about myself at all. I'm only going to help you. I'm going to try and make you happy. That's all I want to do is make you happy. I don't want to see any of you get hurt. I'm scared to leave you. Scared something terrible . . . (Begins to weep) Scared something terrible is going to happen. (Cries) I don't want you to be the kind of people you are. I can't bear to have you the kind of people you are. (Cries bitterly) I want you to be different. (She has revealed her life-style, i.e., to be helpful and responsible for significant others. One terrible thing that did happen in reality is, of course, the suicide of her mother. She is also pressured by her fervent desire that her family be different.)

M. Tell them, "You're all blind." See if that fits. (The statement is an attempt to integrate the dream content with her life.)

B. "You're blind. You're blind. You're blind. Blind people can commit suicide! How can I help when someone is blind? (She starts to realize that she was helpless to prevent her mother's suicide.)

M. Remember that you were seven. How does a seven-year-old little girl feel in this kind of a mess? With two blind parents and a blind brother. You already expressed it. I want you to do it again. What decisions did you make around that age? (She made an important life decision at an early age in regard to responsibility. She needs to discover that decision *before* she can in any way alter her present life-style.)

B. That I was going to take care of them.

M. Exactly. Tell them,"I'm seven years old, and I'm going to take care of you, each one of you."

B. "I'm seven years old and I'm going to take care of you. I want to take care of you . . . Daddy. I'm seven years old and I'm going to take care of you. (Cries) I'm seven years old, Dick. And you're such a great guy and I'm going to take care of you." (Her early life decision is now fully revealed.)

M. I think your dream work is concluded. (Although the dream work is concluded, she realized that there is still hard work ahead of her in overcoming her propensity for being responsible for others.)

B. I think there's still a lot of unfinished stuff there. I've got a lot of things to absorb. I realize the commitment I made.

M. It was quite a commitment for a seven-year-old.

B. But I still felt a sense of failure.

M. Well, of course you felt failure . . . you didn't make it. You didn't save everybody at age seven or subsequently. Your life script now is being a savior.

Chapter II

BODY WORK

INTRODUCTION TO NEO—REICHIAN BODY WORK

Eric H. Marcus, M.D.

The Reichian approach originated from psychoanalytic theory as developed by Wilhelm Reich. Reich held that one's character was a more basic problem than one's neuroses. Consequently, if character armor is first attended to, neurotic traits will then be easier to analyze. Reich correlated his patients' body structure with their character, utilizing psychoanalytic theory; e.g., an "oral" character would have a specific physical structure. At first Reich interpreted to the client what he observed, later he employed physical massage methods to directly alter the muscular armor. Perls was a patient of Reich; however, the contact terminated when Reich left Germany.

Perls emigrated to South Africa, where he practiced psychoanalysis and developed the beginnings of gestalt theory within the framework of psychoanalysis. He returned to Europe to present his views to Freud and his colleagues, but was ignored. He was told, "If you don't believe in psychoanalytic basic principles, then get out of the movement." Perls dropped out, since the scientific method was more important to him than maintaining "belief."

The most direct descendants of Reichs are called "medical orgonamists," the principal disciple being Dr. Ellsworth Baker in New York. The Reichians work sequentially down the body, following Reich's theory of segmental muscular blocks.

There are a number of offshoots from Reichian theory; the best known is the Lowen school, called "bioenergetics." This school emphasizes stress exercises which increase the energy level in order to achieve emotional discharge. Patients are categorized in terms of Freudian psychopathology, which I believe is a disadvantage of this approach. There are other criticisms best described by Malcolm Brown* (e.g., the heavy emphasis on emotional release). I will use a bioenergetic technique when I deem it appropriate even though I do not subscribe to bioenergetic theory.

The Neo-Reichians, such as Malcolm Brown and Charles Kelley, do not use stress exercises primarily; nor do they strictly follow the Reichian segmental approach. They utilize a variety of Reichian *and* non-Reichian methods to foster loosening of character armor.

Rolfing is another type of body work and involves a systematic stretching of the fascae to correct the alignment of the body.

Structural patterning is an offshoot of Rolfing and was started as a post-Rolfing system to perpetuate the results of Rolfing. It involves learning correct ways of standing, sitting, and moving.

The Alexander method and Feldenkrais method are two other body systems, both painless, subtle adjustments of the body which occasionally result in rapid personality changes.

All of these systems are Western forms of body work. Eastern methods were developed over a thousand years ago? Tai Chi and Yoga are examples of body approaches. The Eastern ways have an added dimension. They are paths to attaining higher states of consciousness, while Western body therapies deal only with personality and character "neuroses." With the increasing interest among clients and therapists in achieving higher states of consciousness including the "transcendence" of emotions, the desirability of facilitating emotional discharge is being questioned. The ability to experience higher levels of consciousness is complementary to optimal intra and interpersonal functioning and grounding. Grounding and contact are in large part dependent upon one's body being free from chronic tensions. Thus, Reichian-oriented body work is

---

*Brown, M. A critique of direct body contact therapy, *Psychotherapy: Theory, Research and Practice.* Vol. 10 #2, Summer 1973.

a potent experience in the evolution of one's growth. The lower chakras need to be opened before, or at least simultaneously with, higher chakra development.

A basic concept of Reichian work is "pulsation," i.e., the natural rhythms of the body as expressed, for example, in breathing and sexual movements. Counterpulsations are blocks to natural rhythms, characterized by spasms and tension. The goal of Reichian therapy is the experiencing of pleasure. Reichian removal of the various blocks constitutes the pain experienced during therapy. Pulsations are the flow of "orgone" energy, which Reich considered to be orgastic; however, I prefer to consider it as a general flow of energy.

An important aspect of the body is the state of balance of the autonomic nervous system. The body has two nervous systems, the voluntary and the autonomic. The voluntary controls the muscular movement and skin sensations. The Reichian approach is primarily concerned with the autonomic nervous system, the theory being that character defenses are "automatic," and therefore locked into the autonomic nervous system. This system controls emotions, breathing, and sexual discharge, as well as "psychosomatic" manifestations.

The autonomic nervous system has two components, the sympathetic and parasympathetic. The sympathetic part, sometimes called the "fight or flight" system, will automatically protect you by mobilizing your resources for whichever you choose to do, flight or fight. It will increase your adrenalin, change your breathing pattern, and activate your muscles so that you have increased energy to meet the stress.

The parasympathetic side is the subtler, relaxing side and mediates pleasurable, free-flowing feelings. The goal of Reichian work is to establish an optimum balance in the autonomic nervous system. If, for example, a person is tense and fearful, a change in his breathing pattern will help move him in the parasympathetic direction. If someone has a toneless, apathetic personality and body, a goal would be to energize the sympathetic side.

Frequently body work results in an automatic emotional discharge, character armor thus being progressively dissolved. I am suspicious of vigorous techniques that lead to repeated emotional discharges; I suspect that these involuntary discharges have progressively less psychological importance. I have seen people in body workshops mechanically lying down, doing the stress exercises, thrashing, screaming, and pounding, then getting dressed, going home, and going about their business with no awareness of any connections to their psychological dynamics. However, I am not negating the importance of emotional discharge, since it helps desensitize people to the fear of losing control. That in and of itself is very valuable for loosening character armor.

Body work starts with a general assessment of body structure. To become aware of character armor, I watch for patterns, perhaps not evident the first time the client works. Character armor refers to the way in which a person defends himself. The armor takes many forms—with some it is like a coating of ice, with others, a network of rope. Once I have some idea of the type of character armor, I then have some clues about how to work with that person. For example, if the person's armor consists of intellectualizing, then cognitive approaches are inadvisable. Others may be very creative and fantasize easily, and with them I avoid techniques that lend themselves to "spacing out." Specific indications of muscular armoring include the body's alignment and symmetry. Is the head far forward? Is the pelvis twisted? Is the diaphragm rigid?—and so on.

Reichian-oriented therapists start a session by having the client assume certain specific positions. A bioenergetic therapist would have you do what is called "charging;" i.e., stressful exercises to build up an oxygen charge. A Reichian or Neo-Reichian would have you lie down and breathe deeply. The basic approach is physical, regardless of the psychological dynamics. My own style is to have the client lie down only in specific circumstances. For example, if the person specifically requests body work I won't do it until I explore his motivation. One of my main criteria for using the Reichian horizontal position is if it seems likely that the person may have a deep emotional experience. I don't believe that a sitting position is conducive to expressing deep emotions; it is very easy for a person to curl up and lock himself tighter in his character armor. Even if I eventually do only "pure" gestalt, I'd rather start with the person lying down so I have access to his body.

In preparing for body work, after the client's session has begun I ask if he is willing to work in the Reichian position. If the response is "yes," I observe whether his body language is consistent. I then can be aware of the first sign of resistance; otherwise I'll regret it later. If the person has had no previous experience, I'll say only, "I'd like you to lie on your back." After he lies down I look for evidence of tension. Are his legs held tightly together or crossed? I will ask him to be aware of their position. A beginner may have very little awareness of tension or tightness; his fingers may be clawing the rug totally without awareness. I want a person to be aware of what *is* before suggesting specific actions. I then will ask him to raise his knees up and put his feet flat on the floor. I observe what he does with his knees. (Some women will tightly keep their knees together; the Reichian position may be reminiscent of some traumatic event, e.g., sexual or childbirth.) I then ask the person to place his feet shoulder-width apart. If there is no negative reaction I go on; otherwise I attempt to find the cause of the tension, perhaps a traumatic gynecological examination or a rape. Bringing the knees up takes tension off the abdominal muscles.

I then ask the client to put his hands down at his sides, palms up—this is an open, vulnerable position. I notice whether he figits with his fingers or any other body part, thereby draining off his charge.

At this early stage I am very interested in eye contact and monitoring the degree of trust. If this is the first session I tell him that we won't go any further than he agrees to, I will stop any time he wants, he is not going to lose any more control than he is willing to lose. The more frightened the person is, the more necessity for eye contact. I don't want to work with a panic state; I think panic is a destructive emotion. Panic means that they have lost the observing part of their ego. So if I detect the beginnings of panic, I do nothing but suggest parasympathetic breathing and maintaining consistent eye contact. I am not referring to mild anxiety or fear, that is not the same as panic.

If the person is not panicky and is willing to go further, I then tell him to close his eyes and I watch for eyelid flutter. The more the eyelids flutter, the more residual tension. Some people have so much tension that their eyelids will actually jerk open. If the eyelids are fluttering strongly, I doubt that I'll be able to go deep with the work in that session unless the tension can be somehow reduced.

During the first session I won't touch them without telling them first. I then watch how they react when I do touch them. Do they relax or tighten? If they tighten, they may be in touch with past hurts. I may do some light massage while maintaining eye contact. Their body may be remembering past insults that the mind has forgotten. With very tense or fearful people I might do no more in the first session than to encourage parasympathetic breathing and relaxation in order to give them a pleasant and safe first experience.

Now the real Neo-Reichian work begins—the charging. Charging involves deep breathing so as to change the oxygen/carbon dioxide ratio in the body. The intensity of the subsequent experience is proportional to the extent of the charge. Some people will charge in six breaths while others may take an hour or even longer. An adequate charge is recognized by various bodily sensations, the first indication frequently being tingling in the fingers, face, and sometimes the feet. Numbness, expecially in the hands, is also frequently reported. Color changes may take place, particularly a flushing of the face, and neck, and shoulders.

It is important, especially in the early sessions, that the client not "space out." I occasionally ask the client to look at me and report his awareness. If I am satisfied that he is able to make good contact, I then ask him to close his eyes and resume deep breathing.

As the charge builds, automatic muscular resistances to the increasing energy flow become manifest as muscular contractions, either overt or quite subtle. My first effort is to alleviate the contractions by massage. If this is ineffective, I may then use the gestalt principle of exaggeration, i.e., asking the client to consciously increase the tension.

My personal style is not to do strictly Reichian work; rather, I draw from a variety of approaches at any one moment. For example, any one therapy session may involve a combination of Reichian work, massage, gestalt work, guided imagery, etc. The specific technique I use at any specific moment is a matter of intuition rather than gestalt or Reichian theory. For example, if I observe that the person is not charging well due to "not getting out of the head," I may use guided imagery to engage his head in the process. If, on the other hand, the person is adept at "free association" with imagery, I may then focus predominantly on somatic sensations.

To summarize, the direction of the work is determined by numerous factors, specifically my training in body work as well as intuition, experience, and adeptness with other approaches.

At the conclusion of the session I ask the client to make eye contact with me until I am clearly in focus. I then ask him to slowly sit up and regain his balance and equilibrium. If the work has involved heavy discharge of emotion I will suggest that the person ask for support from one or two group members, which usually consists of quietly being held or being close to them for about five to twenty minutes. Also, if the work has been very emotional I ask the group to refrain from giving feedback until a later time.

The work tapes that follow illustrate the use of Neo-Reichian techniques integrated with gestalt.

TRANSCRIPTS OF NEO-REICHIAN/GESTALT SESSIONS

THE GENESIS OF CHARACTER ARMOR: ISOLATION

An attractive, vivacious woman in her mid twenties has already had a considerable amount of psychotherapy. This work takes place in a group. In spite of initial resistance, she achieves a relatively deep level and faces some painful impasses.

E. My heart is pounding, and I don't want to look at anybody. I'm scared you'll have a hard time. I'm really aware of everybody being here, I don't want anybody around. What I'm scared to work on is how scared I get. I get scared the more responsive the other person is. I need someone to really shake me and I need to go crazy. I'm really tired of this.

M. I don't want to shake you. (Long pause) What's going on?

E. I get really frightened, like someone's going to get me. (Very tiny, small voice) I need to disappear.

M. Stay with that as much as you can. Somebody's going to get you and you have to disappear.

E. It's like they want something from me.

M. Would you be willing to work in the Reichian position? (I anticipate the possibility of strong emotions arising and therefore want access to her muscular armoring.)

E. Yah. (Deep breathing)

M. Breathe at a faster rate. (I encourage "sympathetic" breathing, i.e., stimulation of the sympathetic nervous system, which is the "fight or flight" system. Thus certain stressful emotions are more likely to be aroused.) Let thoughts, images, body sensations, fantasies, whatever, drift in and out of your awareness. (Pause) Tell me the first word that comes to you.

E. "I don't want you near me."

M. Would "Go away" be the same, or "Don't touch me?" (The fewer words, the more impact)

E. "Don't get to me."

M. Let's start with, "Don't." Keep saying, "Don't!"

E. Don't. Don't look so happy. (She elaborates and thereby reduces the potential emotional charge.)

M. Just, "Don't."

E. Don't.

M. Let it build up some power.

E. Don't. Don't. Don't. Don't. Don't. (Breathing deeply)

M. Stay with it. Either use "Don't" or something else, whatever fits. (She does not appear to be increasing her energy charge and therefore I suggest a word of *her* choice.)

E. Stay away! Keep away!

M. Let that get louder.

E. Stay away! Keep away! Don't want anything from me!

M. Say that again.

E. Don't want anything from me!

M. Does this fit, "Don't hurt me?" (I go on my hunch which turns out to be incorrect.)

E. Don't even go near me. Don't even want me. Keep away from me. Stay away.

M. Say that to some people from your childhood. (I want to know which specific persons are involved.)

E. Don't expect anything from me, Daddy. Don't expect anything.

M. Say that again.

E. Don't expect anything.

M. Louder.

E. Don't expect anything!

M. Let it get louder still.

E. Don't expect anything! (Louder)

M. Keep going.

E. Don't expect anything, anything is too much. (Breathing harder) Anything is too much.

M. Stay with that.

E. Anything is too much, I won't give you anything! I won't give you anything, I won't give you anything! (Crying hard) (Really upset) NOTHING, I'LL GIVE YOU NOTHING! NOT A GOD-DAMN! I WON'T GIVE YOU ANYTHING! NOTHING FOR YOU, NOTHING FOR YOU! (Breathing hard)

M. Keep breathing. (Long pause) Do your feet want to do anything? They're moving. If they want to do anything, let them do it.

E. I want to say I'm cold. I'm cold, so don't expect anything from me, 'cause you won't get it. You won't get it from anybody cold. You won't get anything, from anybody cold. (Getting upset again and breathing harder again) I'm cold and I won't go near you! I don't want to go near you! (Crying, sobbing hard, wailing) I don't want to keep you away anymore! (Crying) I want to let you in, but I don't know how anymore. (In a very small, quiet, relatively calm voice) I don't know how to do it. I just freeze and detach myself from my family.

M. Open your eyes. (Pause) I'd like you to decide if there's anybody here, right now, that you would be willing to risk some contact with for a few minutes. (She has defined the impasse—I now bring her back into the present and offer her an experiment to counteract her childhood dilemma.)

E. Chuck.

M. Make contact any way you like. Stay vulnerable and say what you would be willing to risk. (Long pause)

E. To Chuck: I don't want you to get tired of me. I don't want you to be disgusted with me.

M. You're putting things into the negative and also asking for future promises. Can you make positive statements about the now?

E. I'd like you to sit in front of me, that's totally conducive for me not to get scared and there'd be nothing I can get scared of at all. (She sets very definable and conservative limits.)

(Chuck sits in front of her. They make eye contact for about five minutes. I end the work here.)

This traumatic work touched upon a core personality characteristic. In order for lasting and permanent characterological changes, she will need to again and again work in this area, from a variety of directions.

TOO MUCH FOOD

This client has been in a gestalt group for one year, readily trusts me and the group, and quickly gets in touch with childhood experiences. She starts without a focus and then gets in touch with unfinished business regarding her way of eating.

V. My body doesn't feel bad. I feel tense in some places. I feel closed.

M. Let's use the Reichian position. (Since she easily regresses to painful childhood emotional states I want to be prepared by having her lie down so that I can monitor and massage muscular spasms as well as facilitate deep breathing. As her work subsequently progressed, it was unnecessary for me to do any extensive body work to remove muscular armor.)

V. I hesitate to work, because I know I can work a lot deeper now—I'm trusting of you and I'm trusting of the group, and that is scary.

M. Uh-huh.

V. My voice has been really monotone for days.

M. Breathe. (She needs to "charge" herself so that emotional material can surface.)

V. (Breathes deeply in and out) (Breathing becomes a low moan)

M. What do you see or hear?

V. I know lately . . . . I've been aware . . . When I eat, I don't breathe.

M. Breathe.

V. (Breathes deeply) I won't stop to enjoy eating, because I don't like to eat. I eat fast and I get constipated. I hate to eat. I stopped enjoying it and I hate it.

M. When did you stop enjoying food? (She quickly has come up with a specific focus, undoubtedly indicating some unfinished business.)

V. I don't think I've ever liked it.

M. What happened when you were a child with food? (I need specifics in order to develop a focus.)

V. They just made me eat everything.

M. Who's they?

V. My father.

M. Do you remember a scene?

V. Yeah. (Long pause) (Breathing) Right now I'm recalling a conversation I had with my mother a couple of months ago. I started asking her questions about my father. She said that he was a really good father and one thing that really scared her was how he used to always make me eat things. He used to force me, and she was always afraid that was going to bother me.

M. I notice you are doing a lot of shaking and trembling.

V. Uh-huh.

M. Let yourself tremble. (Her muscular armor is melting, as indicated by her trembling. She is coming closer to some emotionally charged material.)

V. (Breathes deeply) I see this tall glass of white milk.

M. Look at the milk.

V. Oh, my head is splitting. (An instantly formed "psychosomatic" symptom!)

M. How old are you?

V. Three. Little. It's . . . (Breathes deeply) . . .

M. What were you going to say?

V. I can't assoc . . . ah . . . like the words don't go with the situation. (The situation may be preverbal.)

M. Are there sounds that go with it? Gestures?

V. (Pause) Ah . . . talking about the situation doesn't fit. Talking as if I am in it.

M. Go ahead.

V. There is so much milk in that glass.

M. Talk like a child. (The more childlike she can talk, the less likely her verbalizations will be intellectual.)

V. It is going to take forever. (Voice shaky—begins crying) There is so much food—God. It is all piled up. (Breathing) It won't fit inside of me. (Begins crying fully) (Cries for a long time) (Breathing deeply while crying) (Her childhood catastrophic fantasy of perhaps bursting from too much food is revealed. Long-repressed emotions are now being released.)

M. Breathe.

V. (Cries fully) IT'S HOT, IT TASTES TERRIBLE! (CRIES) (Takes a long time to calm down and breathes deeply while doing this) Doesn't seem like it should be such an awful experience. I'm really aware I chew my food really fast so I don't have to think about it.

M. I would like you to experiment with some food and be aware of how you chew and eat. (She is back in the present and I want her to experience and integrate present behavior and her childhood traumatic food experience.) There is much in the book *Gestalt Therapy* on eating experiments. Perls said that the way we eat is the way we live. Be aware that your eating style is your lifestyle.

The insight attained from the reexperiencing of her early memory needs to be combined with present-day awareness. Also, experimenting with new ways of eating will broaden her repertoire of eating experiences.

THE HEALING OF AN EARLY DEPRIVATION

This client, a woman in her midtwenties, is easy to work with. The work commences with no focus—starting with her lying in the Reichian position and concentrating on her breathing. After a few minutes I ask her to say the first word that comes to her mind. She says, "Mother."

M. Stay with that word.

G. "Mother, (Crying) Mother." (Breathing heavily)

M. Keep breathing, you're starting to hold. (She breathes deeply.) Stay with the word alone, or add another word or two. (I hope to get some content.)

G. "Mother, Mother." (Crying heavily) She's leaving. (The content emerges.)

M. Tell her not to leave.

G. She won't listen.

M. Tell her that, "Listen to me . . ."

G. "Listen to me, don't leave me, (Crying very hard) you can't leave me!" (Sobbing)

M. How old are you?

G. Eleven (Breathing deeply)

M. When you reach up, you're going to find a hand to hold on to. I want you to try to hold on. She's going to leave slowly. (A physical act usually intensifies the process.)

G. (Crying hard) "NO, don't leave. You can't, you just can't, you can't. DON'T GO, DON'T GO, I NEED YOU. I NEED YOU, I NEED YOU. You can't leave, you can't. (Sobbing) Oh no, I can't let you go, I can't let you go, can't go, you can't go. No, No! (Crying) NO, NO, NO!" (Sobbing—long pause of heavy breathing)

M. Tell her what, if any, decisions about you or others you remember making after she left. (Early decisions are crucial and are the basis of character formation.)

G. I am afraid to be involved, she can lock me out.

M. Tell her what you wish she would have done instead. (The beginning of my efforts to have her positively reexperience this early traumatic event.)

G. "I wish you'd loved us all enough and didn't lock us out. I wish you'd loved me."

M. What could she have done differently when you were eleven? (I need the specifics in order to set up the revised scene.)

G. She could have talked to me.

M. Tell her.

G. "Mommy, you could have talked to me about it, instead of just going."

M. Where did she go?

G. Away.

M. Was there a divorce?

G. It was a separation. I remember overhearing my father and my mother arguing, and her saying that she didn't want the children and she was a Communist.

M. When you're ready, open your eyes. I would like you to pick another "mother," an ideal mother, then be eleven again and have her behave the way you would have liked.

G. (Speaking to "ideal" mother) I'd like you to explain to me, why things aren't working out. That things just aren't going well between Mommy and Daddy, and that's why you're leaving.

M. Go back now to that time as if you could really do it over again.

Mother. "There's something I've got to talk to you about honey. Honey, your daddy and I aren't getting along very well, and I'm not feeling good about it. I'm going to have to go away for a little while, because I need a rest."

G. "You're coming back?"

Mother. "Of course I'm coming back, I'll be back. You know I love you very much and I just need some time to myself. Need to have a little rest and I'll be back. I won't leave you, I'm just going to go for a while."

G. "Promise you'll come back."

Mother. "I promise I'll be back. I love you very much, I just have to have a little time to myself, to think things over. I'll never stop loving you. I hope you understand it's just for a little while."

G. "I'll miss you."

Mother. "I'll miss you too, baby. Tell you what. I'll call you every day. Would you like that? OK, I'll call you every day, you'll get tired of my calling you."

T. "That would be nice, then I'd know you were OK too."

Mother. "Right. What else would you like me to do for you before I go?"

G. "A big hug." (Mother gives it.) That's really nice.

I agree with Albert Pesso, the originator of psychomotor therapy, that following a traumatic event with a positive resolution provides the "healing" factor. Perhaps this is similar to Schiff's "reparenting." This woman's fear of closeness has been successfully challenged by this experience.

Critique by John Stevens: I think this approach is phoney . . . My guess is that J. Schiff doesn't cure her "children," but she is able to teach them how to function in the world despite their psychosis. She seems to be effective—exactly *how* she is effective and whether she *does* what she *thinks* she does is a real question. . . . Giving a "good parent" in place of a bad one *prevents* the client from assimilating and taking responsibility for the part of himself that punishes, stops, threatens, etc.

Marcus response: I believe this is a "which came first, the chicken or the egg?" issue. Steven's emphasis is the primary role of reowning projections, while mine is the primary significance of positive parental experiences. I believe that the client's openness to the reowning of negative projections is dependent upon a secure self-identity engendered by feelings of love and acceptance from parents. The client's punitive top dog represents an introjection, and the removal of that introjection can only take place from a position of basic self-worth. I believe that the reowning of negative projections per se, without this prerequisite, is a superficial process. I have seen numerous examples of client's acceptance of their negative traits *after* the establishment of self-love and trust.

A SEARCH FOR MEANINGFULNESS

This work took place as the client lay in the Neo-Reichian position. His opening remarks made me suspect that strong feelings might emerge, and therefore I had him lie on his back. After closing his eyes and breathing deeply for a few minutes, I asked him what he was aware of. He said he felt scared. I asked him to keep repeating, "I'm scared."

M. Switch to the word "Don't."

J. Don't! Don't! Don't! Don't!

M. Follow "Don't" with another word.

J. Talk. Don't talk. Don't talk. (Breathes deeply)

M. Who are you talking to?

J. Myself.

M. What are you scared of?

J. The unknown. Darkness.

M. How old are you now? Are you scared of the dark? (He probably has gotten in touch with himself at a very early age.)

J. Three. Alone in my room. The light's on in the hall. I'm alone and afraid of the dark.

M. Where are your parents?

J. My mother's gone someplace, and my father is in another room.

M. Be that little scared kid. Think out loud.

J. I'm in the darkness and I can see the light out in the hall. I don't want to be alone. I want to be recognized. I want people to know I'm there. I want them to know I'm awake and not asleep. I want them to know I exist. I can see the light. I want attention.

M. How do you want to get it?

J. I want them to *know* that I'm there.

M. How can you make them know that?

J. I make noises.

M. Go ahead. Be the little kid. Get attention.

J. (Coughs. Groans. Clears throat loudly. Groans more.) I'm here! I'm here! If the phone rings and it's for me, don't tell them I'm asleep or I'm not here.

M. You're three years old? (I am skeptical. Three-year-olds usually don't get phone calls!)

J. Yes, yes. I want someone to call for me, call me on the phone. When the phone rings I hope it's for me. I hope it'll be for me. I want to be acknowledged.

M. Stay with the words, "I am" for awhile, if it feels good for you.

J. I am. I am. I AM! *I* AM!

M. Keep going.

J. I am! I am. I am. I am. (Weakening) I am. (Loudly) *I AM!!* (Weeps) Help me. I am. I AM. I AM! I AM!!! (Weeps bitterly)

M. Let the sound out—whatever sound is coming.

J. I am. (Some groaning) (Heavy weeping) I am. I am! (In control) I am. (Weakly) I am. (Crying) I am. I want you to know I am. (Laughter mixed with weeping) I just want to . . . (Inaudible—mixed with crying) Shit! Shit, shit, shit! Fuck! (Continues to cry and words don't get out) Shit! I fucking am!

M. Make them hear you. (Encouraging him to express his anger fully)

J. I am. I FUCKING AM!!! I AM!!! (Cries continuously) I am. I know. I can't . . . I'm so tired of it. Shit, shitshitshit. (Begins to calm down) That's what's been and that's what will be. (Continues to cry) I can't believe how far . . . fucking ever. Oh, God. Oh, shit. (Makes sounds of words, but they don't get out) Shit. Terrible. I don't understand . . . I fucking don't understand it. SHIT! Oh, fuck.

M. Take deep breaths, bring the air all the way in. (His excitation is waning. By encouraging deep breathing, he may regain his "charge.")

J. (Attempts to do so) (Long silence) (He is calm and quiet, then begins to weep again) The lights are out. It's just a good way for what I see. I see ahead. (Begins to cry bitterly again) Oh, shit! (Can't get words out) I have to make my own light or realize that time and time again, this takes so much energy. (Calming down) And I feel disappointed because it seems so artificial. . . . Instead of making anything in life . . . it should be there. Life should be. Should be meaningful. (Sighs)

M. You have a choice. Either make your own meaning in life or subscribe to somebody else's meaning.

J. Yeah. I know. I choose . . . to make my own, it's just that I'm so tired . . .

M. If things get too rough you can join Hare Krishna or something . . .

J. (Laughs) I will.

M. All you'd have to do is learn two words and your troubles are over! (Lots of laughter)

J. I feel a lot better I've forgotten this. I've fucking forgotten it.

M. There's a lot of shit buried inside.

J. I feel like a stranger that just arrived in town.

M. Welcome.

J. I wonder what I'll do now. Wonder what I'll do in the new town. What'll I see first? Where will I go?

M. You have a welcoming committee here. (Laughter)

J. It's a welcome sight. I feel good, bad, or whatever. I want to go see the sights.

Although his work was brief, it was exceedingly potent. His character armor was softened by this powerful experience. Nevertheless, he will need considerable follow-up work to effect permanent changes in his personality.

THE ANGRY JAW

This man, in his early thirties, has had previous experience in Reichian therapy. The work shows the connection between character (muscular) armor and personality traits.

G. I'm experiencing a lot of tightness in my jaws and my whole face is a lot of sensations, the last couple of days. Feeling pressure last night in the eyes. Noticed I was doing a lot of chewing, biting my lips. I don't know what to do with it. (I now ask him to lie down and breathe deeply, hoping that using the Reichian approach will get to emotional conflicts.) (Deep breathing)

M. As you breathe, be aware if anything specific comes to you; a word, a memory, a feeling, or a sensation.

G. (Pause) My eyes.

M. Say something about your eye.

G. The light's in my eyes. My eyes are jerking. (Breathing) My head is full. (Breathing)

M. Say that again. (A possible focus)

G. My eyes aren't seeing. (Breathing) My eyes are wet. (Breathing) My head is full. (Breathing)

M. Let a sound come out when you exhale.

G. (Breathing with ooooaaaaas several times)

M. Bring your lower jaw forward, make a sound when you exhale. (Another potential focus and potentially more significant than his eyes)

G. AAAAAAAAAAHHHHHHHHHHS (Begins to sound almost like a growl and gradually gets louder and more growlish, then like a suppressed scream getting louder and louder and turning into a cry) (Lighter breathing as in rest, relief) My jaw feels very loose.

M. I should hope so! (Laughter)

G. I feel good. I'm really relaxed.

M. (I manipulate his jaw.) That's really hard, if you feel your own jaw, you'll be surprised how still it is. Notice, you can hardly move it unless you really give in.

G. I feel like a board, usually. (Breathing)

M. Do you know what your sounds were all about? (If possible, I prefer to relate an emotion to some content.)

G. No, nothing there, just that. (Pause) My eyes feel teary, but I don't feel sad at all.

M. Make up sentences starting with the words, "My aggression . . ." and let anything pop out, even if it doesn't make any sense. (My hunch is that his aggression is being blocked.)

G. My aggression hurts. My aggression . . .

M. Stay in eye contact. (Eye contact prevents him from intellectualizing and also keeps open an avenue for expressing his aggression.)

G. My aggression feels good. My aggression scares me. My aggression is mean. My aggression is eyes. My aggression is teeth. My aggression is in my jaw. My aggression is shaking.

M. Change it to, "What I do with my aggression is . . ."

G. What I do with my aggression is bite.

M. (Massaging his jaw muscles) The tightness is in these muscles You constrict them and keep your aggressive feelings inside you. Practice keeping it loose by letting your jaw hang slack. Another thing to do is to be aware of people or situations that you feel chronic anger about, that you keep inside, and grit your teeth.

G. Yes for the last month or so I've been sometimes waking up grinding my teeth.

Although he did not get in touch with any specific content for his anger, he was nevertheless able to release some muscular armor. Although the Reichians don't stress the cognitive element, I believe that in order for lasting change, a cognitive element is necessary. Accordingly, I advised him to become aware of instances of anger with his concomitant muscular tensing.

WRITER'S BLOCK

A screen writer in his late twenties complains of a block in his creative ability. He appears very tense and I decide to work with him using Neo-Reichian methods rather than gestalt. I ask him to lie down and breath deeply. He remains tense and fidgety, with numerous muscular motions throughout his body.

M. I'm going to suggest something that may or may not be possible for you. See if you can consolidate all the energy from the different parts of your body. (Long pause)

J. (Very loud breathing)

M. Now can you gradually and progressively loosen your jaw. That way the energy will flow and not get trapped.

J. (Continues and makes the sound, "Ahhh") (The sound "ah" vibrates the larynx and loosens throat muscles.)

M. You mig t experiment with a different sound. Make an "O," like ooooooh. (The "o" sound will vibrate and resonate the upper chest.)

J. (Does it)

M. Do it only as long as you feel good, don't force. (Pause) Now I'd like you to start some sentences with the words, "I am . . ." and add only one word.

J. I am relaxed, I am relaxed, I am good, I am unblocked. (Pause and light breathing) Unblocked from all over.

M. I imagined your body before as a mass of short circuits. Everything vibrating and jerking, uncoordinated twitches. Now you've got your body together.

J. Um, it feels unified. I feel pretty narrow.

M. Do you feel like writing right now?

J. I feel the desire to, but I don't want to right now.

(The work concludes for now. On an organic level, he has integrated his body and his energy flows. In a subsequent session the following week he reported no further difficulties in writing.)

Chapter III

GUIDED IMAGERY

GUIDED IMAGERY: AN OVERVIEW

Silvia R. Marcus, M.A.

Guided imagery (also called guided fantasy or guided daydream) is a tool which can be appropriately used within any theoretical framework. In this work the client allows images to appear on his "mind's screen," and the guide (therapist) then takes the client on a "trip." Robert Desoille (5), Hanscarl Leuner (12), and Joseph Shorr (13-16) have developed systems of therapy based on imaging. Psychosynthesis uses guided imagery as one of its major tools.

Robert Assagioli (1) considers imagination as a psychological function. As such it can be exercised and developed, thus increasing the creativity potential. Imagination, since it operates at the levels of sensation, feeling, thinking, and intuition, has an integrative effect; it simultaneously uses right and left brain functions. Imagery makes use of subjective symbolism, thus bypasses the rational mind and makes areas "safe" which the client may otherwise be reluctant to face. Images tend to produce the physical conditions and the external acts corresponding to them. A wide use of this principle is easily observed in the advertising industry. In therapy, a simple use of this fact is to ask the client to visualize a symbol for a given quality (such as patience or determination), then have him draw this symbol and post it where he will see it many times a day (usually I recommend the refrigerator door!).

The sensation aspect of imagery (visualization, auditory evocation, and the other senses) can be developed by exercises. Assagioli (1) describes several of these in *Psychosynthesis*. Choosing numbers or shapes and colors (e.g., a red triangle) and then visualizing them is a simple and effective concentration exercise. Similar exercises for the other senses are to "remember" the smells of familiar objects (such as fruits), to hear familiar sounds, to taste familiar foods. In this training, the basic process is to be able to bring about the desired imagery at will. This develops the repertory for spontaneous imagery work, much the same way that stretch exercises develop the elasticity of the body. These exercises also strengthen the will as well as concentration and attention.

The feeling aspect of imagery is emphasized by the client being encouraged to be in touch with feelings. The thinking process materializes through the verbal sharing of the imagery.

The imagination function ranges from the concentration exercises to the free flow of images (such as the "active imagination" of Jung (11)). In the middle range falls guided imagery work. Guided imagery can also be used as a projective test for diagnostic purposes (Leuner (12) and Shorr (13-14)) and as a systematic desensitization technique, in which the subject is repeatedly taken safely and slowly through a phobic-related trip.

Another effective use of guided imagery is with somatic symptoms. I ask the person to see himself very small and to go inside his body (he can either go alone or take someone with him, or call on someone at any time he wants). I ask for a description of where he is entering, how he is traveling, and what he is seeing along the way. The trip itself is very different with each client and even on repeated trips with the same client. Sometimes it is very symbolic, like fixing electric equipment or cleaning filters; at times there are encounters with past or present situations (which may reinforce the theory that different parts of the body contain their own memories). At the end of the trip I am careful to bring the person "out" and resume his normal size.

It is usually advisable for the client to be in a relaxed state (accomplished through any induction technique) and in a comfortable, lying-down position. I have done guided imagery sessions without this preparation, however, and it has worked out well also. Some people can go easily into their imagination and others require the preparatory relaxation. Once the subject is suitably relaxed, the session starts. The state of relaxation is such that the subject is not in a trance; it is important for him to retain consciousness in order to remember all that happens. Recording the session for future listening is of great value.

In beginning the work, Leuner (12) suggests giving the client a starting theme, such as a meadow, climbing a mountain, or following a brook upstream to its source or down to the ocean. These starting themes are for diagnostic purposes and therapy. For diagnostic purposes he suggests keeping in mind the quality of the different themes, the factors that inhibit progress with the given tasks, the incompatibility of situations (such as a refrigerator with no food), and the nature of the emerging symbolic figures and their behavior.

Joseph Shorr (13-16) has developed a therapy using imagery, which includes an evaluation test. He presents the subject with an image from one of several categories and the client proceeds with his imagination to complete the "story." Some of the categories are: Dual imagery (go down the hall, there are two doors facing each other, open each door); task imagery (go up 1000 steps); body imagery (sensing yourself from head to toes, what is the body part of your identity); sexual imagery (imagine an animal emerging from a penis and one from a vagina, have them walk down a road together); self-imagery (there are two of you: one in a cave and one outside—imagine the outside one going in the cave); spontaneous imagery. Questions asked with each imagery are: What do you see?, What do you feel?, and What do you do?

Desoille's (5) starting themes are systematic and purposeful. He has six themes, including: to confront one's obvious characteristics (for a man a sword, for a woman a vase); to confront one's suppressed characteristics (descent into the depths of the ocean); and so on. Desoille deals extensively with the symbolism of the guided fantasy.

Other possible starting themes, most of which originated in Psychosynthesis, are: a door with a name of an emotion written on it; images from nature (such as a forest or a journey to the center of the earth); animals; a meeting with a wise person; a scene from a dream; a symbolic image of a life situation, somatic pain, or feeling; a drawing; or any image the guide or the subject may present.

In general, ascent trips (such as climbing a mountain or going to the sun) result in positive strengthening experiences, including those of mystical qualities. Descent trips (such as going to the bottom of the ocean) explore the deep areas of the personality. "The goal is to bring to the surface from the depths and to the valley from the heights, in order to integrate both and to extract what is of value for everyday experience" (Gerard: Lecture).

Once the session is in process the guide intervenes with varying degrees of directiveness. The less directive the guide is, the more the subject strengthens his ability to cope. In general, I am more directive with a beginner in this type of therapy than with an experienced client. Suggestions such as: "Are you willing to go halfway?" may encourage the subject to take risks. Interventions of a general nature include asking the subject to describe scenes, feelings, and actions, thereby sharpening the focus. If the subject is stuck, ask him to stay with the image and see what develops, as if watching a movie. Asking the subject to be the "observer," to describe what is happening as seen from the "outside," can bring new energy to a stuck situation. A non-directive, useful question is, "What is going on now?"

Suitable techniques during the session vary widely. The client can be asked to have a dialog with and/or between the people in the fantasy, with and/or between objects in the fantasy, and between people and objects in the fantasy; to explore a situation (such as a dark room, a cave, a house); to become (owning) symbols in the fantasy (be the door); to make friends with "enemies" or "monsters" (owning the dark side). Or the guide may select any other appropriate technique with which he is acquainted. In dialoguing and making friends with enemies, questions such as: "What do you want?," "What can I give you?," "What can you give me?" are useful to clear and resolve conflicts. Usually the action will come to a natural resolution, at which point the session concludes. If time runs out, the guide can suggest that the subject come to a temporary conclusion. Working at the symbolic level is per se therapeutic. It is nevertheless very important for the client to translate the symbols and symbolic actions into everyday life. If immediate association to the symbols does not occur, a productive "homework" is for the client to become aware of associations in the following days. Journal writing and art work enhance the therapeutic value of a session.

Subjective symbolism does not have *rational* explanations or interpretations; attempting to make the symbolism rational will deprive it of its subjective meanings and effects. Rational explanations are not to be confused with relating the symbolic action to real life. For example, if a person sees himself flying in the Universe among the stars as part of his fantasy and attempts to explain the flying mechanism, that will deprive him of his feelings of freedom and take him into an intellectual exercise. The connection with reality comes about when he relates his feelings of freedom to life situations where he feels locked in.

Once conflicts have been cleared, the new position can be rehearsed in the imagination. Assagioli (1) refers to this process as the "Ideal Model Technique." The person images himself as if the desired change has already taken place, practicing this as a daily mental exercise. The change can be a body image (see oneself slim), the acquiring of a quality (such as humor or strength), a specific behavior with a given person, or a change in attitude (seeing oneself holding an infant with love, which is also oneself). Usually there is a time lag between imagery changes and physical reality changes and some people (guides as well as clients) are impatient. The fact is that, in spite of their impatience, changes do occur in due time when the person has faith in the process.

Concluding this article is a brief bibliography of guided imagery books and articles. Crampton (2) and Elliot (6) have written detailed historical backgrounds of guided imagery and their works include more extensive bibliographies. A new Journal of Mental Imagery (17) is now being published.

I do not recommend that an inexperienced therapist do guided imagery. This method is very powerful since the subject is in a highly suggestible and vulnerable position, thus trusting the guide for a safe journey. More than with some other methods, the experience of being a client, as well as proper training, is extremely important in order for the therapist to use guided imagery safely and productively.

EXCERPTS FROM A SESSION

(C: Client. S: Silvia. Internal thoughts in parentheses)

C: Everything is going wrong. My checks from welfare are not correct, I'm not doing well in school . . . (about 5 minutes of listing all that's wrong).

S: (Silent. Let her do her complaining until a focus develops.)

C: (Some more complaining) . . . It's like I am in a deep hole in the earth, very dark, and I see the light above, but every time I try to climb, I slide back down.

S: (With this analogy I see a good opportunity to go into guided fantasy). Close your eyes and be in that hole—describe it.

C: Smooth walls, very deep.

S. How did you try to get out?

C: By digging in the walls and putting my feet in, but I slide back down and the holes get smoothed out again.

S: How else could you get out?

C: I don't know.

S: (Several attempts lead nowhere). Imagine a sun in the middle of your chest and the warmth and light from that sun spreading all through your body.

C: (Pause). O.K.

S: Now, in your mind's eye, open your eyes and look around.

C: It is lighter now.

S: Do you see any other way you can get out?

C: For a flash second I saw a door.

S: Do you see it now?

C: No, it's behind the wall.

S: Talk to the door and ask how to get to it.

C: Door, how can I get to you?

Door: You have to find out by yourself.

S. (Again, several attempts lead no place). O.K. Sit in front of the door and imagine a sun above your head, your Higher Self. See that sun connected by a shaft of light to the one in your chest. Now talk to your Higher Self and ask for guidance (an attempt to have her find out by herself how to get to the door).

C. Would you help me?

H.S.: You have to do it by yourself.

C. It is very hard for me to get in touch with my Higher Self. She won't talk to me.

S: (One more attempt at internal guidance meets with same results.)

C: . . . It feels like I could go even deeper.

S: Do that, go as deep as you can (might as well go down since she is obviously not ready to go up. I'll take her as far down as she'll go and see what happens).

C: When you said that, the floor gave in and I am much lower.

S: Describe where you are now.

C: It's a very small place, just big enough for me to be here. I feel protected with the earth around me.

S: (I asked for more description of what she termed a cave). Talk to Earth.

C: I feel protected here, I don't want to go out there.

Earth: Yes, that's what you do, you either hide or you expose yourself totally.

C: I want to hide. When I go out there, it is like a storm and I am a tree and my branches get broken.

E: When you go out, you go out roots and all.

C: What do you suggest I do?

E: That you keep the roots in the ground all the time, even when the storms come.

C: Yes, that is a good idea.

S: (This dialog went on for a few minutes along the above lines until it started to become redundant). Can you see yourself as the tree?

C: Yes.

S: Describe yourself.

C: Short, bushy tree. The roots . . . there is one center root, very strong, the rest have not had a chance to grow (the client is short and heavy).

S: Where are you, as a tree?

C: On a hill, not very high, a view around and a patch of grass.

S: (I ask for a few more details of the place and the tree.) Pick a place where you want to be as a tree and tell me where that is.

C: It's on the patch of grass.

S: See yourself there, then, and see your root system starting to grow. Can you see that?

C: (Pause) Yes.

S: (At this point I see a good opportunity to integrate the protection element from the cave and the nourishment element as a tree with a healthy root system.) Now, get in touch with the feeling of protection you had when in your cave.

C: (Pause) O.K.

S: I would like you to go back and forth with your feelings of protection in the cave and of nourishment as a tree with a root system that is starting to grow and be strong and healthy. Let me know when you experience that.

C: (Pause) . . . Yes.

S: Stay with that for a while and when you feel that you can go there any time you want come back to this room by opening your eyes. (Pause . . . client opens eyes). Well, I suggest you use that last part of your fantasy as a daily meditation for the next week, maybe twice a day.

C: That feels very good.

S: I want to point out to you that YOU did that; that this is YOUR meditation; that YOU made it up. I only put the pieces together for you. (Today, and in past sessions, the issue of "I have to do it myself" is very strong, so I am emphasizing that she, in actuality, gave herself the means).

C: Yes, that's right! I thought I was copping out by going in the cave.

S: Well, that is a possibility, but going in the cave is protection for you and you want that protection right now, so use it! At the same time you can be the tree developing a root system that will keep you from being thrown all over when a storm comes.

C: Yes, I can see that now.

S: Meditate overlapping the cave and the tree, so you get the feelings of protection and nourishment from Earth. And, by the way, Earth seems to be your inner voice connection, so when you want guidance, go to your cave and talk to Earth (it is important to point out the positive aspects of the client's symbolisms and to remind her that *she* is the author).

Note: At the beginning of the session, the client *seemed* to want to come out of her hole. Soon it was apparent that only intellectually did she want out, that emotionally she wanted to stay in. Following where she *was*, rather than where she *wanted* to be, was the crucial move, for she then realized the value of the protection she received in the cave. This gave her enough strength to come out as a tree. In this form, the same source of protection, Earth, was able to nourish her.

In our next session I recommended she draw the cave and the tree on the hill and post the drawings. This reinforces the effects of her symbolism.

BIBLIOGRAPHY

1. Assagioli, Roberto: *Psychosynthesis.* Viking Press, Inc. NY 1971.
2. Crampton, Martha: *A Historical Survey of Mental Imagery Techniques in Psychotherapy and Description of the Dialogic Imaginal Integration Method.* Quebec Center for Psycho-Synthesis, Inc.
3. Crampton, Martha: The Use of Mental Imagery in Psychosynthesis. *Journal of Humanistic Psychology*, Fall 1969.
4. Crampton, Martha: The Aerial View: Some Techniques for Facilitating Objective Perception. Psychosynthesis in Research Foundation, Inc., New York.
5. Desoille, Robert: The Directed Daydream. Psychosynthesis Research Foundation, Inc., New York, 1966.

6. Elliot, James: Personal Growth Through Guided Imagery. Explorations Institute, P.O. Box 1254, Berkeley, CA 94701.
7. Freundlich, David, M.D.: Fantasy Approaches in Psychotherapy: The Guided Fantasy, (304 W. 105th St., New York, NY 10025).
8. Gerard, Robert: Psychosynthesis: A Psychotherapy for the Whole Man. Psychosynthesis Research Foundation, Inc., New York, 1961.
9. Gerard, Robert: Symbolic Apperception and Integral Psychology. *Psychotherapy and Psychosomatics*, 1974.
10. Gerard, Robert: Symbolic Visualization: A Method of Psychosynthesis. Psychosynthesis Research Foundation, Inc. NY.
11. Jung, C. G.: *Analytic Psychology: Its Theory and Practice.* Vintage Books, 1970.
12. Leuner, Hanscarl: Guided Affective Imagery. *American Journal of Psychotherapy*, Vol. XXIII, No. 1. January, 1969.
13. Shorr, Joseph E: *Psycho-Imagination Therapy.* Intercontinental Medical Books Corp., 1972.
14. Shorr, Joseph E: The Use of Task Imagery as Therapy. *Psychotherapy: Theory, Research and Practice.* Vol. 12, No. 2, Summer 1975. (588 S. San Vicente Blvd., Los Angeles, CA 90048).
15. Shorr, Joseph E.: *Psychotherapy Through Imagery.* Intercontinental Medical Books Corp., 1972.
16. Shorr, Joseph E.: *Go See the Movie in Your Head.* Popular Library, 1977.
17. *Journal of Mental Imagery*, Vol. 1, No. 1, Spring 1977. Brandon House Inc., P. O. Box 240, Bronx, NY 10471.

COMMENTS ON THE USE OF GUIDED IMAGERY

Eric H. Marcus, M.D.

I have found guided imagery techniques especially valuable with intellectually defended beginners. Since they are "in the head" anyway, I employ their head as an ally in fantasy work.

Sometimes I use imagery work for conflict resolution, working symbolically. I may ask the client to imagine a split screen and simultaneously see both sides of an issue on the screen. As they watch the "movie," the conflict frequently becomes resolved.

Imagery work is useful in providing a time perspective. For example, if the client cannot decide whether to get a divorce, I may say, "It's two years from now and you've gotten the divorce." And then, "It's two years from now and you have not divorced." They will present their projections and frequently achieve more clarity about the relevant decision.

Another use of guided imagery is to encourage a stream of consciousness. This is good with people who don't give themselves permission to be illogical. Many times the stream of consciousness leads to some previously unrecognized unfinished business.

Guided imagery can be very potent when applied to psychosomatic symptoms. I have the client travel throughout his body—going to the ulcer or the headache—and symbolically "fix" the disturbing organs, with consequent symptom relief.

Another large area suited for the use of guided imagery is the "transpersonal;" i.e., the spiritual dimension. Imagery methods are utilized extensively in most Asian philosophies to achieve higher consciousness.

There are some contraindications to the use of guided imagery. I don't use it if the client is very anxious; the lack of concentration produces meandering. I don't recommend its use with people who are very poorly grounded; i.e., the psychotic, the borderline personality, the severely hysteric. I don't recommend it with persons who have a "flight of ideas;" they can indefinitely jump from image to image.

Guided imagery work in a group requires caution because of the length and intimacy of the work, which may bore the rest of the group. I have been surprised a number of times when I thought the work would be brief only to find it extending considerably. The following work tapes illustrate the use of guided imagery with gestalt.

TRANSCRIPTS OF GUIDED IMAGERY/GESTALT SESSIONS

GUIDED IMAGERY AND ASTHMA

This work illustrates the use of guided imagery. The client explores a symptom and eventually arrives at the locus of the difficulty.

N. My chest is a large issue with me, not just because of the tightness I feel sometimes but there's an ongoing thing too with drugs. I've been taking cortisone for three years now . . . I want to get rid of that tightness without the use of so much drugs . . . without the use of cortisone.

M. I want to work with a technique called "guided fantasy." Lie down and get comfortable. Then miniaturize both of us and decide by what portal of entry we get in.

N. . . . into my mouth.

M. All right. Describe the journey; the two of us are going to take a journey into your lungs.

N. I'll just take you by the hand and we can walk down my tongue. And when we get to the back of my tongue, my throat often is . . . you can see some white . . . a little bit of white. It never seems perfectly clear. A lot of times I have a little soreness there; I can go for months with just a little bit of soreness . . .

M. What do we see and feel as we go down?

N. There's a lot of secretion . . . it's kind of gooey. And It's getting darker. As we get down we get to the top of the lungs . . . there's a lot of mucous membrane and it's pretty active. And the passageways are small because the muscles tighten up a lot so we're gonna have to squeeze down. And sometimes it's inflamed and it's tight and gooey. We can just sort of slide through the place or something.

M. Where are we going? What are we heading for?

N. I'd like to head down—way down deep. I have the imagery about the upper part, but I don't have much about down below, so we can go down and see what's going on down there. I have a little flashlight . . . It looks . . .

M. Any areas that we haven't explored? That are still dark?

N. I'm beginning to feel they're all the same; it's a pretty complex network.

M. Guide me to the area that seems to be in control of the whole system. (We are not yet at the core of the trouble.)

N. *Here* is where I'm most aware of. This seems to be an initiating area because things tend to flow down.

M. Okay, so take me to that area . . .

N. There's a lot of mucous-secreting membrane there.

M. Let's get closer into the membrane. What's the membrane look like?

N. Whitish. Pinkish-white. Sticky.

M. Let's get really close so that we can eventually get in and find out what the hell is going on.

N. There's chemicals that probably should be here that aren't here. That's why they're like they are. That's what I feel. (Apparently the trouble is the absence rather than the presence of some factor.)

M. Some missing chemicals?

N. Yeah.

M. Where would they come from?

N. They should come from some other part of my body, but they're not getting there.

M. What part of the body?

N. I think it's adrenalin.

M. Where would that come from?

N. I think it comes from my adrenal cortex.

M. All right. How are we going to get there?

N. MMMmmm. That's tough . . . to get there from here.

M. Well, I imagine it would be through the blood. (I am impatient and offer him a "travel" suggestion.)

N. Yeah.

M. Maybe there's some other way you'd rather go. (I regret my suggestion and therefore offer him alternatives.)

N. I guess the blood would be the way to go there.

M. All right. So we go through the heart and eventually get to the adrenal cortex. Upon our arrival, what do we see?

N. It's got cobwebs on it. There's cobwebs. It's not working.

M. Go on. Take me into that area.

N. And it's rusty. It's all shut down. And it's not being used. It's been out of use for a long time.

M. Is there something the two of us can do to get things going again? Clean up the place? (Again I am impatient and prematurely offer a suggestion.)

N. Break chairs.

M. Break chairs? What does that do? (He apparently has very different goals in mind than I had!)

N. That makes it work. Just . . . start breaking chairs. Just pick up a chair and smash it down on the floor really hard . . . (Pause) . . . That . . . makes it work for a little while.

M. What about the rust and the cobwebs? Is that significant? Do we have to take care of that or will that take care of itself? (Apparently I am still interested in cleaning up the place.)

N. It's significant . . . that breaking chairs only gets the machine to work for a little while. It's a very temporary kind of a thing. I guess the rust and cobwebs need to be taken care of. (Perhaps breaking chairs represents the expression of anger.)

M. Let's attend to that. (Long pause)

N. Well, it seems like it's going to be more than that too. It looks clean now, but I don't have faith that it's really going to make the difference. The rust and cobwebs are gone but the machine is just . . . sitting there, and I'm not convinced it's going to do anything. It just looks better.

M. We need to explore the machine. What's wrong with it?

N. Maybe it's got some missing parts. Maybe it's never been used.

M. Can you locate the parts that are missing? Identify what's wrong . . . what's missing? (Perhaps the missing parts are the clue to his difficulty.)

N. Input. It needs input.

M. What kind of . . . parts need to be put in?

N. It needs an electric input.

M. Oh! So then the parts are okay . . . and you're saying it needs some current?

N. Yeah, it needs current.

M. Where would the current come from?

N. Wires. It needs wires. I have a feeling it's never been wired. We've got to make connections from my sense receptors down to the adrenal cortex. They've . . . gotta go through another place before they go from the receptors to the adrenal cortex.

M. Where's that?

N. There's some kind of evaluation, some kind of screen that's needed.

M. Is the screen there or do we have to put it in?

N. It's in my head. (Hopefully we have finally arrived at the source of his difficulty.)

M. All right. So, let's take a quick trip up there and see what's going on.

N. I'm confused now, because I'm not sure . . . maybe the screen has been too effective . . . maybe the screen is the block.

M. Maybe the screen is so thick that it may actually be filtering so that no electricity gets down.

N. I think that's where the problem is.

M. What does that screen look like?

N. It's all clogged. Nothing gets through. The wires go from the receptors to the screen, but then they . . . things don't get past the screen.

M. What needs to be done to rectify the situation?

N. Clean out the screen.

M. How do we do that?

N. There's a lot of stuff on it. Probably . . . removing it and shaking it out. We'll take the screen out and just really shake it around and get rid of the stuff.

M. Do that with your hands now. Reach up to the screen. Shake some of the crap off it. (N does so.) (By involving him physically the impact will be greater.)

N. I don't want to put it back in 'til it's clean. Or I'll have to put it back in and keep taking it out once in a while to keep working on it. I can't get it all clean. All at once. (This hints that his work for the time being is over.)

M. Is it okay if we put it back now? Even somewhat cleaner?

N. I want to give it one more shake. (Does so) We . . . can put it back for awhile. I don't feel it's cleaned off.

M. Is some current, though, getting through? (I hope that something has been accomplished.)

N. I hope so.

M. Put the screen back and see what happens to the circuit.

N. (Does so) Some current gets through now.

M. Maybe we better see if the machinery is starting to move.

N. It's moving, but it seems like it's unsure if what it's doing is right.

M. It hasn't been running for a long time. (An attempt to connect the imagery with his chronic symptoms)

N. Yeah.

M. It's going to take awhile to really get into a routine.

N. Yeah.

M. I think that's all we can do for now . . . we'll have to go back in and do some more work on the filter. (Setting the stage for future work)

N. Yeah.

This work was rather laborious—patiently following his path of "causality." The style utilized here was to stay with symbolic imagery throughout, rather than interspersing connections to psychological dynamics. Approximately three months after this work occurred I received a letter from him indicating that his symptoms had markedly decreased.

AN EARLY DECISION TO BE WORTHLESS

This work illustrates the use of guided imagery with gestalt. The woman is an easy client to work with; i.e., her defenses are not too great and she has easy access to her emotions.

V. One thing I'm very aware of is that when I came in and sat next to you, I wanted to cling to you. I wanted to cling to somebody I trusted. I feel afraid, I'm going through a lot of pain . . . and I've experienced it before. I had a boyfriend last September and decided not to see him anymore. I went through about two months of pain—it was just awful. And now I'm doing it again—this guy I've been seeing in the last couple months, I decided not to see him, and it's awful. (Restraining tears) It doesn't seem that it's just going through pain—I've gone through pain, but some kind of block that's . . . horrifying.

M. Okay. I'd like to continue with you lying down. (I ask her to lie down in the Neo-Reichian position because I anticipate that she will become increasingly emotional and she is less likely to block her feelings while lying on her back and breathing deeply.)

V. Okay. (Sighs many times, breathing deeply)

M. See if you can get in touch with the pain—if you're not already. Breathe deeply.

V. (Breathes deeply) I feel it *here.* (Indicating her abdomen)

M. Good. Stay with it. If you can don't fight it. Go into it and see where it takes you. (Staying with a physical symptom is a way of quickly getting to the essence of whatever is going on.)

V. (Breathes deeply) (Begins to cry)

M. Stay with it.

V. (Continues crying more heavily)

M. Deeper.

V. (Cries more)

M. What is happening to the pain?

V. It feels deep.

M. Are there any images that come to you?

V. (Begins crying again) These two sides are fighting with each other.

M. What are they fighting about?

V. One side says, "You're not worth anything" . . . and that's the side I *really believe.* I really am worthless! The other side is not real, it's phony. Then I see it's dark. (Sighs) Those two are trying to distract me from something in the dark.

M. Keep breathing. Stay in touch with the dark.

V. (Cries bitterly) I want to see it! I can't! I feel ready to see it . . .

M. Don't rush. When you're ready, you'll see it. Whatever the "it" is.

V. It looks like a door. (Long pause)

M. Go on.

V. It's got a sort of foggy glass with texture in it. You can't see through it. The door is wood—like a school door from an old school. All around the door there's no walls—it's just dark. And when I look at the dark, it's real deep, and . . . I feel despair and depression. When I look at the door I feel . . . it's safe . . . but I'm pretending it's safe. (Sighs) I don't want to look at the dark, so I look at the door there. I hear some people inside but I can't see them. They're . . . two men teachers, and they're talking to each other about me.

M. What are they saying about you?

V. They're saying, "We both care about her. What are we going to do? (Begins to cry again) What are we going to do?" I'm little. I'm really young and they're old.

M. How little are you—about? (I am checking whether she has made a connection between the fantasy and an early memory.)

V. I don't know. But I'm sitting in a chair where my feet can't reach the floor. (Laughing)

M. What's little Vicky been doing that's gotten the teachers to their frame of mind?

V. I don't know, but I feel that they care . . . they're sincere, they're really talking about how to help me, not how to punish me. (Crying)

M. Talk to them in your fantasy.

V. I don't think they know I can hear 'em. (Laughing slightly) I don't want them to know that I can hear 'em. This way I can hear more!

M. Okay. Hear some more. What do they say about you?

V. (Begins crying heavily again) They're saying, "How can we help her? She has to go back, and there's nothing we can do, but we care. We can't take her home because she's not ours. We can't do anything because she's only here a couple hours a day. She's always (practically whispered) going to feel worthless."

M. Say that again. (She has made a key statement about her self-image and I want her to be really aware of it.)

V. She's always going to feel worthless. That's just the way she is. (Cries and sighs) I don't understand what they mean. They know something about me . . .

M. More than *you* know?

V. Uh-huh. They know I'm going to have trouble later.

M. Listen some more. What do they say about you and your background and your situation? (I want more information.)

V. (Crying) They feel kind of sorry for me, because I don't have a father. They want to be my father. They want to care . . . (Sighs) They say, "Her mother can't give her enough." They have a lot of authority, they're wearing suits and they're educated and . . . they're not just doing their job.

M. If they could, what would they like to do?

V. They'd like to make me secure. They'd like to make me feel good about myself. (Cries again) But *nobody* can. *Ever.* I keep getting in trouble, or things keep happening. I keep coming back to the same chair, and the same thing—I'm no good. Something's *missing.* (Sighs)

M. Let's reprogram and start from the beginning of the scene and this time put in what's missing. Change the situation. (An early negative experience can be neutralized by reliving the experience in a favorable way.)

V. (Cries) I know what it is.

M. What is it?

V. (Cries bitterly) I don't want to think it! I don't want to think it! (Calms herself) I really want them to do the impossible. I really want them to take me home and be part of their family. I know it can't happen, and I don't want to think it!

M. It can't happen in real life. It can happen in a fantasy trip. (Events transpiring during the guided fantasy have a greater than realized impact upon "real" life.)

V. It scares me. (Pause) I don't want to think that . . . if I know it can never happen, I don't want to want it so much.

M. The way not to want to want it so much is to go with it and get it out of your system . . . (A key concept in gestalt therapy is not to resist what *is*. By going *with* rather than resisting, the impulse abates.)

V. I'm afraid it's going to feel too good! (Laughs) I feel that something terrible's going to happen if I do it.

M. It's only a fantasy—a dream.

V. It's the same way now.

M. Say that again. (Key statements are emphasized by having the client repeat the statement.)

V. It's the same way now—my life. I don't want to want to so bad.

M. My hunch is that if you reprogram that fantasy, things may go better for you in the "now" world.

V. Yeah. I want to let go of the tightness. (Sighs) (Breathes deeply)

M. You are trembling. Let the trembling go. (Long pause)

V. I'm sinking. Feel like (Laughs) nothing's holding me together. (She is now "giving up"—she feels no support.)

V. Nothing's holding me together. It's like spreading all out. (Laughs) (Long pause) (She emerged from this impasse with a very pleasant feeling.)

V. Somehow that touches everything. (Long pause)

M. I have mixed feelings about whether to let you relax and

enjoy—and hold redoing your fantasy for some other time, or whether to go ahead with it.

I decide to leave well enough alone and let her enjoy her euphoric feelings at this time. Naturally, *all* of her feelings of insecurity and inadequacy are not resolved by this one work, and yet she has taken an important step.

THE LION AND THE BOSS

A woman in her midtwenties has a conflict with her superior on the job and cannot decide whether to quit or not. This work is almost entirely by means of guided imagery and shows how to work with symbolic projected elements.

B. I don't want to go back to work. I resigned my job, it's because this lady I work with hates me so much and I have to hear her go through all her rejections of me. I've already gone through being angry with her. First I was depressed, so I got all that out, and I'm feeling like I don't want to go back to work. I need the job really bad to stay in school. I don't know how to handle her.

M. I'd like you to picture the following scene as if you were watching it on a screen. Tell the rest of the story. The scene is this woman meeting a lion. Describe what you see. (The lion frequently represents the projected anger.)

B. She's trying to act really cool and she's scared to death. She's trying to scare the lion, before the lion can scare her. The lion is believing her. They're walking around in an arena and she's putting on a big show and a lot of people (representing her co-workers) are watching her and they're not quite sure if they'd rather go with her, because she can talk, and the lion can't. (Her feelings of impotence)

M. What happens next?

B. The lion, I sort of sense what the lion's thinking, the lion's thinking, "Why can't all those people see her shaking, and she says she's not scared!" It's a beautiful animal and it's obvious to me that I'm (she substitutes "I" for the lion, indicating her identification) winning, but I can't talk and I don't want to play even if I could talk, I wouldn't want to do what she's doing. I would just be getting more and more into a game. I'd rather be just a beautiful lion. (Long pause)

M. Continue the scene.

B. People in the audience are looking back and forth between the lion and her, like a ping-pong game. They don't say anything, they won't get involved. (Long pause) The lion is getting anxious because he wants them to do something. (Pause and breathing heavily)

M. See what happens next.

B. The lion is getting really mad, he has no way to fight her and the audience is just apathetic. He's really frustrated, just running around in a circle, saying, "There's no way to communicate with this woman, she lies and they know she lies, she lies to them." (The impasse deepens.) The lion doesn't understand anything. (Starting to cry) A couple of people from the audience come over to talk to the lion. They tell him, "You look like you're going to leave. But you're going to meet other people like her, you're just avoiding it." The lion says, "I know it's right for me." They want the lion to take responsibility and do something. He doesn't know how to. (Crying) She (Changing the lion's sex) doesn't want to go, she wants to stay, but she doesn't know how to play the game. (Crying) Three years, learning how to be a lion. (Referring to her years in psychotherapy) (Crying) I want someone to help me. (An impasse: environmental support or self-support?) (Sobbing)

M. Who are you in the scene? (I want confirmation as to her role.)

B. I'm the lion. This woman's going to crack. I don't want to wait for her to crack, it'll kill her. I don't want to be in that game of waiting for her to kill herself or do something awful, because this is her whole life. How the hell am I going to get out of this. I can stay here, I'm just tense, I'm not doing anybody any good, I'm not doing myself any good. I'm in total frustration.

M. Watch the scene, see what the lion decides to do. (I offer her no way out of the impasse.)

B. He's getting sad and he's just sitting there too.

M. What happens next?

B. It's just a stalemate, nothing can happen.

M. Is the audience looking at the arena? (Perhaps the impasse will be broken by means of the audience.)

B. They're still not doing anything. The lion is getting sad. The lion realizes it's really a beautiful animal and then it gets angry with the audience and angry with everybody, but they don't have any expression on their faces. The lion is sad and it wants to leave.

M. What does the lion decide to do?

B. It wants to go to you. (I imagine she expects me to get her out of the impasse.)

M. Where am I in that scene?

B. You're in a room, but you don't have anything to do with what's going on. You're talking on the phone and doing some sort of work in an office.

M. And the lion wants in?

B. I know you can't help me. There's nothing you can do. I don't even want answers from you, because I know there aren't any. (I am relieved that she has this insight.)

M. I'm willing to go back out to the arena and sit there. (Giving her some support)

B. I'd like that. Now I'm not alone, the lion's not alone.

M. Where am I sitting in the arena?

B. You're sitting right next to the lion. You're saying, "Hey, what are we going to do now?" And the lion is saying, "I don't know, I've been working on this for such a long time. I always thought the answers were in me, but this time I don't know." You're saying, "I'm here and we're going to see what we can do." And the lion doesn't feel alone anymore. It's stuck.

M. What do I tell you, what do I decide to do?

B. You're saying, "The people in the audience don't know what they're doing. (Pause) They're going to wait and look over the situation. They don't want to get involved. They don't want to lose anything." (A statement about her coworkers)

M. Watch the scene and say what happens next.

B. The lion says, "I don't want to be involved with these kinds of people. I know another world of real people and I don't want to have a life like this, even if I have to be put in a zoo, I'll still be a lion. If I stay here, they're going to want to cut my hair and make me ugly."

M. What does the lion do or say next?

B. If the lion goes, they're just going to get somebody else to fit it, it's going to be barren and it's never going to be good for anything but the people right there. The lion doesn't have the tools to fight them. The lion's saying, "At least I feel OK, I know what I'm feeling." The lion doesn't feel the struggling any more.

M. How does the scene end?

B. The lion's in the zoo and he's not doing what he wants to do, he's got to spend a lot of time just being there, it's going to be a long time before he gets out. He feels good on the inside, it's not where he is that makes him feel good or the kind of work he has to do. (The impasse is resolved. The zoo represents returning to school.)

M. The good thing comes from inside, you're saying, rather than the environment?

B. Yah, he's in bars, but he's peaceful; someday I'll be able to be out, someday I'll be able to do what I want, someday I'll be able to finish school. The lion is saying that right now it's peaceful and I can enjoy the people that come by even though it's not exactly what I want. (She is reconciled to the situation and thereby relieved of tension.) I was afraid that was going to happen. I don't feel bad about leaving. It's just going to take me longer to get where I want to be. This is the first time I've made a decision on my feelings; I've always done the "rational" thing. My stomach feels really relaxed.

M. Your agitation has stopped; you had been agitated most of the time. When you're ready, look around and come back to the group. (Pause)

B. I feel very responsible for myself. Like I've taken care of myself. A good feeling. And that's sort of a precedent.

This long piece of work, done entirely at a symbolic level, illustrates one means of impasse resolution. Grounding, however, is important—grounding, in this instance, means relating the imagery work to the person's daily life. Within one week after this session, the client terminated her job.

DESCENT INTO A WHIRLPOOL

This woman undergoes a very intense guided fantasy experience. She has just finished relating a very detailed, lengthy dream. The work illustrates Perls's concept of the implosion layer of the neurosis.

M. What are you in touch with right now?

C. Anxiety.

M. Stay in touch with your anxiety.

C. (Long silence)

M. See if you can "enter" into your anxiety. (Instead of dealing with any part of the dream, I am curious about her anxiety.)

C. It's like a whirlpool that's pulling me down faster and faster. I'm on the outer edge and as I am sucked down I go faster and faster and get deeper and deeper. It is dark in here.

M. See what happens next. (I did not expect her to enter into a fantasy; however since she did, I go along with her.)

C. It's darker and darker and colder and colder and deeper and deeper. (Long silence) And as it gets darker and darker and colder and colder, the other aspects of anxiety recede. (Long pause) It's like if I go all the way to the bottom of the whirlpool, that will be IT.

M. I would like you to lie down and then continue. (She has been sitting. I anticipate that she may get into strong emotions and I would rather proceed with her lying down so that she can breathe more fully as well as be amenable to Neo-Reichian work.) (She lies down.) Go wherever you feel safe in regard to the whirlpool. Get as close to it as is comfortable for you. (To allay her initial anxiety, I want to minimize the risk.)

C. I'm right on the edge—moving—slowly, and I can feel the sound of the water rushing around.

M. Imagine that I can give you immunity from harm. Some sort of magical power that will allow you to go down into your whirlpool and come back completely unharmed, unscathed. (By means of "magic" she may grant herself permission to explore deeper material.)

C. (Crying) Well, . . . I go down. Oh, it's getting small; but it's getting faster and I'm getting dizzy. It's getting darker and darker and the roars become so loud that it's louder and louder and now I am deafened. I no longer hear the roar, and now all I see is this blackness and the cold. The blackness is the blackness of nothingness. But the cold is . . . it's colder and colder. (Long silence) It's nothing. It's like I cease to be.

M. Explore it for as long as you want. (I don't want her to rush through a space that may be very significant.)

C. It's not really a bad feeling. It's no feeling. Just cold. Ah, I think I'll look up and see if I can see any sign of light and where I came from. I see a little sliver, a part of a circle of just a tiny, tiny glimmer, tiny, tiny. And it's far, far up. It's like looking at the stars—far, far, far. But there's no sound, just that tiny glimmer of light. I can't see anything from where I am up to that first glimmer. Although, I know I came down on the whirlpool of water.

M. Would you like to get closer to the light? (Some encouragement to begin her ascent)

C. (Long silence) Um, I don't know how. I can't fantasize a way back. The whirlpool is whirling me in one direction and to get back to that glimmer, I'll have to go against it. (She anticipates resistance.)

M. You may need some sort of propulsion system or something. (Supporting her by offering her the opportunity to provide herself with assistance)

C. Yeah, I guess I would grow some flippers on my feet (Pause) But it is very, very hard. I'll see if I can go back up. But, oooh, it is so hard I'm physically exhausted. I go half a turn and I slide back, and another half a turn and I'm flipping with all my strength.

It's like the water keeps pushing me back down. I am trying to go up and it looks just as far away as it did before.

M. You may need bigger flippers to change the balance. (Additional support is offered.)

C. Yeah, I need those professional two-foot jobs. Yeah, that's what I need. Maybe a little jet motor on the back of my heels. Oh! But it's so hard! I'm moving, I'm aware that I am moving. There's no sound. I am moving in a circular fashion and I am gradually going up. But, oh! oh! it is so hard, cause if I stop for a moment to rest, I slide back. It's a continuous fight. It doesn't look quite as far away as it did. I really want to go all the way up now. I feel like I am getting my second breath. I feel like I got a second wind. It is easier now, and it is going faster. Even though I am aware that the water is against me, it is exciting now. It's fun now, it's great, it's a thrill! I'm fighting the water; but I am making progress. I'm coming up and up! It's like it's only a hundred yards away. Only five or six more times around the whirlpool. The force of the water seems to be decreasing, it seems to be slowing down. It seems to be offering less and less resistance. Now the water has a color. And it's a dark deep midnight blue. And it is becoming warmer. It's really fun now. I am really enjoying it! I am enjoying going around and around and around. The water is getting a lighter and lighter blue and now it's aquamarine. I am really going fast. I mean I've never swum so fast in my life. Wow . . . here I am. I'm on top! (She laughs.) (Long silence) Wow! That was neat! If you hadn't been there, I might have decided to stay at the bottom, because I really wasn't having any bad feelings at the bottom.

M. You have gotten used to solitude a long time ago. You can tolerate those situations, those empty houses, empty spaces, etc. (She had previously mentioned her lonely childhood during which she learned to cope by tolerating "emptiness." Her descent and subsequent exhilarating ascent provided her with a novel experience in contrast to her comfortable place of no feelings.)

Chapter IV

PSYCHODRAMATIC METHODS

"CLASSIC" GESTALT & PSYCHODRAMATIC METHODS: A COMPARISON & CRITIQUE

Eric H. Marcus, M.D.

I have found the use of certain psychodramatic methods especially valuable in the resolution of unfinished business, in contrast to "classical" gestalt work, which involves the client's playing the role of others so as to elicit and then reown projections. In general, psychodrama is improvisational role playing by group members. I rarely do this, since the improvisational material often reflects projections of the role players rather than the client, and therefore confuses and complicates the situation. To avoid the contaminating influence of projections, I prefer the innovative methods of Albert Pesso (1). Pesso uses group members as "accommodators," i.e., to act out only and precisely whatever the client wishes. In this way all roles, actions, and interactions are exclusively the projections of the client.

When I use Pesso's psychodramatic methods the work usually progresses through several stages.

First, a conflict (unfinished business) with a significant person is identified. Second, whatever emotions have been repressed are expressed, the client thus learning that the expression of strong emotions is not disastrous. The third stage involves making implicit demands explicit (e.g., "I demand you love me!").

Next occurs the impasse—the realization that the other will not (or did not) yield to the demands. The resolution of the impasse occurs when (if) the client exercises self-support. Self-support can take several different forms. First, the demands may be terminated; for example, "I really don't want (need) . . . from you anymore." Or it can lead to another (more important) aspect of self-support, the establishment of a functional self-identity. ("I can like me, I am likeable, I can love me, I do love me. I can meet my own demands.") A third form of self-support is the realization that the demands may be met by someone other than the original person, i.e., in the here and now. To summarize, demands based on past experience are contended with in the present.

In my opinion, the fifth step in the resolution of the (original) unfinished business is the symbolic gratification of the original demand. The client is now ready to experience and assimilate the gratification originally denied. This is a very important learning experience, since the client is now learning the value of direct, nonmanipulative requests. This step should not be taken prematurely, that is, while the client is still involved in manipulative behavior.

The vital and final sixth step is the internalization of the love and acceptance feelings received from others, so that continual external reinforcement becomes unnecessary. This occurs first within the context of the psychodrama, then within the unstructured context of the group. Thus the bridge between the "there and then" and the "here and now."

The gestalt method for resolution of interpersonal conflicts is by means of identification and reowning of projections. The process involves development of the capacity to distinguish between the reality of significant others and what has been projected onto them. The next step involves the acknowledgment and reowning of projections, leading to the development of compassion, both for self and others.

I find that the "classical" gestalt method frequently involves little emotional expression in comparison with psychodramatic methods. Also missing is the focus on the formation of new positive relationships. Fortunately, many gestalt therapists have incorporated meaningful group interaction into their style.

In summary, the reowning of projections constitutes the *process* of the work, the *content* being self-acceptance. The client's reowning of projections is not in and of itself sufficient if the process has been primarily intellectual. The key issue is how to reown projections on a truly experiential level. One potent means is by utilizing interactions with the therapist and/or group. By means of experimenting with new behavior, the client experiences the *consequences* of the reowned projections. For example, if the projection was negative, catastrophic fantasies do not come to pass. If the projection was positive, feedback reinforces this position.

Even though I personally do not use the role-playing type of psychodrama as originated by Moreno, I want to respond to Dublin's (2) critique, namely that it is a nonresponsible, manipulative method. I agree with Perls's definition of a healthy individual as one who has given up manipulation and is self-supporting. To have a "supporting cast" within a psychodrama does not per se constitute manipulation, any more so than a gestalt therapist's requesting a client to change chairs is manipulative.

Dublin also makes the point that the gestalt therapist's interventions must be too frequent and too concerned with organic minutae for an orthodox psychodramatic approach. This is certainly valid. However, what is the objection to unorthodox psychodrama and/or unorthodox gestalt?

Dublin's claim that the gestalt therapist " . . . continually brings to his (the client's) attention all observed attempts, emotionally or behaviorally to attenuate his experience . . ." is impossible practically. The therapist, rather, selects *some* of the client's behavior, based upon the therapist's own foreground. What the therapist chooses to focus on reflects the style and expertise of each individual therapist, *not* gestalt theory.

To conclude, I agree with the Polsters (3) that, "Although both Perls and Moreno might disagree, we believe that this is primarily a difference in style rather than in theory. Perls believed that since each of the roles was only a projection of parts of the individual, nobody else could play these parts. Nevertheless, projection or no, there is still a world out there—and it is capable of ever-changing configurations and susceptible to a variety of interpretations."

My hope is that gestalt practitioners avoid orthodoxy and continue to integrate other approaches within the gestalt theoretical framework. Gestalt theory, per se, is an integration of Western and Eastern philosophies.

The remaining chapters in this section are transcripts of gestalt sessions utilizing psychodramatic methods.

BIBLIOGRAPHY

1. Pesso, Albert, *Movement in Psychotherapy*, New York University Press, N.Y., 1969.
2. Dublin, James, "*Gestalt Therapy, Existential-Gestalt Therapy and/versus "Perls-ism" in the Growing Edge of Gestalt Therapy*, Smith, Edward, Brunner/Mazel Publishers, New York, 1976, p. 130.
3. Polster, Erving & Miriam, *Gestalt Therapy Integrated*, Brunner/Mazel Publishers, New York, 1973, p. 316.

TRANSCRIPTS OF PSYCHODRAMA/GESTALT SESSIONS

SUCH A GOOD BOY!

My question is a very unusual "opener" for a therapy encounter. It is of course much more customary to ask what the person would like to focus on. In this particular situation I had a hunch that the client was very reluctant to have a gestalt experience with me.

M. Is there anything in particular that you'd like to avoid?

C. Yes.

M. What would you like to avoid?

C. Feeling frightened. Making the decision. Taking a stand. To go somewhere.

M. Don't change position. Just be aware of your hands.

C. Uh hum. I know that my hands are there. They're there purposely.

M. Tell us. What's the purpose? I'm curious.

C. My feet are cold and I sneeze from cold allergies so I try to keep them warm. No, it's true. That's why I usually wear shoes.

M. That's not what the gestalt theory says about all that. That's the way it is.

C. I'll have to change doctors then.

M. In addition to that, see what else they were going to say. But it's too late now, you've let go (of his feet).

C. No, it's just to keep warm, really. My feet are very cold. They always are when I don't have shoes on.

M. Does this sentence fit? "Right now I have very cold feet."

C. Yes, in many ways.

M. Try it.

C. Right now I have cold feet, I'm scared. I'm very tense. My mouth is dry.

M. My guess is that you are prepared, today in your work, to suffer. And feel pain. My hunch is that you are girding and that you have prepared yourself during the week to come here and do that.

C. No. I have a fear that . . . something occurred two weeks ago that has never happened in my life . . . to that extent . . . and it frightens me. I was even afraid to talk last week. The word is even blocked out. The word suicide heightens it.

M. What's the "it?"

C. This fear, this great emotional thing that happened two weeks ago. I was unconsolable.

M. You keep talking about it but you haven't said what it is.

C. Uh. Two weeks ago I was transferred to another assignment. It meant the end of my personal ambition for a higher or an administrative position—the end of a ten-year fight . . . which was my ambition, not theirs. And I realized it was coming but I refused to acknowledge it until it occurred.

If a situation is unfinished it means that there are unresolved emotions (either positive or negative) attached. An unresolved conflict or situation will prevent the person from utilizing his full energy. I was attempting to find any connection between his emotional turmoil and prior unfinished business.

M. Let me ask you, is that situation unfinished for you at this time?

C. No. Well, it's resolved. Yes.

M. And what do you want with me in telling the story?

C. Well, the same day my wife and I decided—well, should you move out or should I? For all practical purposes, I have no other family. I have a brother but he's dead and so am I to him. Everything was gone there was . . . I was going to lose my child . . .

I still do not have a clear idea as to where to focus my attention. He has thus far presented two very distinct *possible* areas of conflict.

M. Again, what do you want to do with that at this time? Let me ask you another question . . . Is that finished or unfinished?

C. It's finished. I'm upswinging but it scared me so much that I don't know if I were to go back to something like that whether I wouldn't give up. It scared me that much.

M. Well, what would you like right now?

C. Strength, I think. Ah . . . courage. I gave up, Eric, two weeks ago. I was ready to read the whole world off.

M. All of your statements are in the past, Curt.

C. OK.

M. And it's sort of an endless recitation of history. I am getting lost as to what you want from me now. Twice I've asked you if something was finished and you said, yes, it's finished. I need more of a now type of contract with you.

C. (Coughs) I honestly don't know what . . . I can do or want to do. I feel like a scared little kid.

M. Say that again.

C. I feel like a scared little kid.

M. Are you willing to go with that?

C. Yes.

M. Close your eyes and be that scared little kid part of you. (Pause) Without words, with just a nod of your head . . . and take your time . . . indicate to us when you are in touch . . .when you have something specific, something major . . .

The client is in touch with a very specific feeling. I am attempting to find out whether he can connect the present feeling with any past unfinished business.

C. (Nods)

M. What age of a scared little kid are you?

C. Ten.

M. What's happening?

C. I just got beat up for the first time in my life . . . the only time . . . by four or five black kids. I was terrified. I came home . . .

M. I come home . . . mention it in the present . . . I am coming home . . .

C. I come home and say, Mom, I just got beat up, I'm scared; I'm hurt.

M. What happens next?

C. She washes my face and then says, you're OK, forget about it, and then leaves.

M. What do you feel?

C. Alone, like there's no one to protect anybody . . . and I can't trust people. I couldn't trust the guy who beat me up not to do it again. I couldn't trust my mom.

M. Feel that . . . see if you can get into the state you were in at that time . . . say something . . . stay at that age and relate at that age and say something to your mother . . . call to her or something . . . if you could have done it over again in a different way.

C. Hey, Mom, stop cooking and sit down with me . . . talk to me.

(Co-therapist takes part of Curt's Mom . . . indicated by CT when she speaks)

CT. Gotta cook dinner now, Curt, you're OK.

C. I'm not really. Mom, it's important.

CT. I have to get dinner ready here . . . you're OK now. I washed it off. You got beat up . . .

C. I want you to stop that, Mom. Talk to me and sit down. Stop it. . . . If you don't stop that, Mom I'm going to take that and throw it on the damn ground. I mean it.

CT. Curt, you're kinda upset, you got beat up . . .

C. Stop it, now.

CT. I gotta get dinner ready here.

C. I don't give a damn. Stop now. (Pause) You aren't going to stop, are you?

M. Make her listen.

CT. I gotta get the dinner ready and I have a lot of things to take care of, Curt, I don't have time to talk.

C. Mom, this is very important. I don't know if I can go back to school tomorrow.

CT. Oh, Curt, come on . . . You'll be OK tomorrow. I've got to get busy and take care of the house so why don't you run along and find something to do.

C. No. When do I come first instead of last?

M. You're getting into your adult life (from tone of voice) . . . try to stay with your ten-year-old as much as possible.

C. I'm important, Mom, you've gotta listen to what I have to say.

CT. Not right now, Curt, I have to get dinner ready. You're OK, I know you've been beat up, but you'll be OK.

C. (Sigh) I'm not ten anymore. I just want to hurt that old lady.

M. Stay with the words "pay attention to me."

C. (Coughing) Mom, would you take five minutes and sit down, please?

M. Pay attention to me.

C. Pay attention to me.

CT. I'm very busy now, Curt.

C. I need something now. I don't know if you can give it, but I need it right now.

M. Say that again.

Important statements are emphasized by asking the client to repeat them. The client is usually so caught up in his work that statements of particular importance may not be given emphasis; accordingly I ask clients to repeat those statements.

C. I don't know if you can give it, but I need it now.

CT. I gotta get dinner on the table now, Curt.

M. Stay with it. Let yourself experience your power in demanding this.

C. Huh. (Sighing)

M. What's happening? (Some cushions are put behind him.)

C. I'm starting to sweat . . . Mom, I've never yelled at you.

CT. I hope you're a good boy, Curt.

C. I'm not supposed to. I'm supposed to never yell, I'm supposed to do what you say, but I've got to have you . . . (Sigh) . . . talk to me. It's important.

CT. Not now, Curt, I'm fixing dinner.

C. (Sigh) (Pause)

M. Go ahead, make her hear you.

C. (Sigh) What do I have to do for you to hear me? Do you hear me at all? Are you listening?

CT. You see, right now it's dinner time.

C. I can't scream and yell at her.

M. Well, lose control.

C. My whole history, well, forget it, head stuff.

M. Lose control.

C. I'd better not. If I do I get clobbered . . . I've been clobbered.

CT. Who clobbered you?

C. My father. And worse. I followed every order.

M. Now is the chance to reverse some of that and experience things that you never dared to experience.

I am now proposing that the client reexperience some original situation in a new way. This is one way of finishing the unfinished business. It is a way of "reprogramming."

C. (Big sigh)

M. CT will be your mother and she won't give you the satisfaction of a reply.

CT. Just be a good boy, Curt, and you'll be OK. I can't talk, son, I'm busy right now.

C. (Sigh)

M. Take your watch off before you get started.

CT. Be a good boy, Curt, don't make a lot of trouble.

C. I never make trouble.

CT. That's right, that's my boy. You're my good boy who doesn't make noise. Just don't make trouble and you'll be OK. Take care of yourself . . .

C. (Yells) Shut up, shut up, shut up.

CT. Such a good boy, talking to his mother like that . . .

C. You don't give a shit about me, you don't give a shit . . . you don't give one rotten shit about me.

CT. (Constantly giving good-boy conversation in a very low voice)

C. You don't care. My brother doesn't care. My father doesn't care. He's not good. When he dies, I'm going to laugh.

M. (In a role) I'm glad you've calmed down and going to talk about it instead of . . . I thought for a minute you were going to get upset and do something to the pillow, but I'm glad that you've decided just to calm down instead. We can always talk things out.

CT. Right. As long as everybody is reasonable, in time . . . don't get too upset about things, I hate to see people upset . . .

C. We can't talk, goddamnit, we can't talk . . .

M. Just watch what you're doing . . . calm down, we can talk, just settle down.

CT. Keep your voice down.

C. (Monotone, constantly while M and CT are talking.) We can't talk, we can't talk, we can't talk . . . (Louder and louder) We can't talk . . .

M. Keep your voice down, (etc.)

C. No, no, no, no, no . . .

M. Knock it off, for goodness sakes . . . Just like those other kids at school . . .

CT. It's terrible, our son has been such a good boy . . .

C. I'm nobody, I'm nothing.

M. Keep that up and you'll go to prison . . .

CT. Settle down, Curt you're such a good boy . . .

C. (Calming down)

CT. That's it, just calm down and you'll be OK.

C. I can't fight you.

CT. You won't.

C. I won't fight you.

M. (Open again) Are you aware of that distinction?

C. Yes.

M. I imagine that for most people that you just went underground. And you developed your own style.

By "style" I mean character. The therapeutic task, of course, is to facilitate the client into loosening his character, i.e., style, and develop a flexibility.

C. I've developed a lousy style. I can't yell.

CT. Won't.

C. I don't yell. I won't get mad.

M. OK. I want you to do one more thing. I'd like you to stay with that sentence, I won't get mad. I want you to say it ten times. Each time you say it I want you to slap the cushion, and look at Mother and tell her, "I won't get mad."

What I am doing, of course, is to present the client with a paradox. The paradox will increase the psychological pressure within him and hopefully result in weakening his character armor, i.e., allowing himself to get angry.

C. I won't get mad (slap). I won't get mad. (Continuing with greater force)

M. Stay in eye contact, look at Mother.

C. I won't get mad (Slap, etc., ten times). I hate your fucking guts.

M. Tell her some sentences starting with, "What I've done with my anger is . . ."

C. What I've done with my anger is to hide it, to push it down, to become a freak. What I've done with my anger is make myself afraid to feel. What I've done with my anger is to make me someone I don't want to be. What I've done with my anger is to make my image of a good guy, and I don't like it and I don't want to live with it. What I've done with my anger is to screw up my whole life and waste good energy on shit.

M. OK then. Satisfied? Take a look around the group just to reestablish contact.

C. I feel for the first time that I've released part of me and I feel good.

Not only has the client been able to release pent-up anger, but the release also begins to loosen his character armor and consequently his need to maintain a "good guy" self-image.

YOU'RE A PIG, UNCLE!

Using a minimal amount of psychodrama, this client does some intensive work on a longstanding undesirable trait. He is very intellectual and prefers to articulately discuss his difficulties.

R. I am aware that I don't chew my food as thoroughly as I would like, and I rush it down and swallow it rapidly. I'm sort of intellectually aware of why I do that.

M. Spare us the reasons. (Laughter) (Hopefully thwarting any lengthy explanations)

R. It has to do with an uncle who used to visit; who when I was a child was really a pig. I'm afraid he's going to take the food and that I'm not going to get any. I'm not sure if it's an intellectualized reason.

M. What are you feeling right now? (An abrupt switch in focus as an attempt to elicit feelings rather than continue listening to his narration.)

R. Anxious.

M. I'm thinking of a psychodrama about you and your uncle.

(The dramatic impact of a psychodrama may elicit his suppressed emotions.)

R. As a child I would be periodically descended on by this uncle who is really a pig.

M. Pick a "pig."

R. There's nobody here that really fits, but Michael . . .? (Laughter) Since you're the biggest.

M. Structure it a bit more. (The more realistic the scene, the more the impact. Especially important are the physical positions of the persons involved.)

R. You would be sitting here, probably, and I would be sitting here. And it's not really that there's not enough food, because there was always really enough food. But it probably has something to do with the kind of food and the quality and various things about the food. And I feel that I have to compete with you because you eat very rapidly, and you just kind of do it with both hands. Yeah, you eat very rapidly, I get very angry at you, but I don't ever express any anger because that's not proper.

M. Do you have food?

R. Yeah, I have food, and everyone has food, but I feel somehow competitive.

M. This (giving him an apple) will be your food. Close your eyes. (Thereby enabling him to concentrate on the situation) (Sounds of eating)

M. Eat a little faster.

R. "Hey, (to uncle) why don't you slow down eating?"

U. (Uncle) I'm eating very slowly.

R. "You know, you're really a pig! You're really a pig! No shit! You really are. You come here and you're eating . . . you're really a pig! You're such a fucking pig! I really dislike you!"

U. "Wow, this is really great!"

R. "Why don't you take a bath? You're really a pig!"

U. "Mmmm, fantastic!" (Makes eating noises)

R. "You don't chew your fucking food, you don't eat . . . you're really a pig. Why don't you leave and just not come back? Leave . . . Just get the fuck out of *my* house! And don't come back and don't disturb *me!* Pig . . . You come here and you freeload! You're a pig!" (Long silence)

R. I feel okay. I have an awful lot of anger toward this particular man that I never was allowed to express and the one time that I expressed being angry toward him I was reprimanded.

M. My hunch is that your anger is partly expressed but there's still some.

R. Yeah, right.

M. Stay with "You're a pig!" and really get loud.

R. "You are really a pig! A pig! You're really a pig!" I feel . . . disgusted. I'm really disgusted and wanting to withdraw. I'm not really angry. Just disgusted. Yich. You pig! Barf! What a pig! (His anger has changed to disgust.)

M. As a finale I would like you to eat something and experience different ways of chewing. One of Perls's experiments is to chew food to the point of liquefaction. If you do that for six weeks, eating habits will change for the rest of your life. Your whole taste for food will change. Perls wrote about the chewing process and digestion and that how you chew is very representative of your life-style.

The client has undergone an emotional experience as well as made a cognitive connection with an unfinished situation. I suggest some homework for him to discover additional aspects of his eating habits.

Critique by John Stevens: What is missing in this psychodrama is the client's realization that he is the pig, he is the glutton who shovels down food without tasting it. I see the anger as only the first step. If he becomes the pig he can realize this part of himself. Psychodrama prevents this unless it allows for role-switching.

Marcus response: One issue here is the selection of foregrounds, i.e., the focusing upon a significant area. In this work I selected the client's retroflected anger as my foreground. ("I don't ever express any anger because that's not proper.") By the conclusion of the work he states, "I have a lot of anger . . . that I was never allowed to express and the one time that I expressed being angry . . . I was reprimanded." The psychodramatic structure catalyzed the release of his retroflected anger. At the conclusion of this work he states, "I'm not really angry, just disgusted . . ." By moving through his anger he made contact with a primary emotion, disgust. The capacity to express disgust is critical in the development of the ability to reject introjects as well as to appropriately assimilate new experiences.

Having the client get in touch with the pig part of himself is certainly valid. One of my concerns is that the reowning of his pig could be an intellectual process, since he has already stated at the beginning of his work, "I'm sort of intellectually aware of why I do that." Assuming that his realization is truly experiential, what then? The gestalt is *not* complete until the original unexpressed anger is attended to.

To summarize, it is my opinion that effective character change comes about by a combination of: cognitive awareness, reowning of projections, *and* the completion of emotionally charged unfinished business.

APPRECIATING THE NEGATIVE

This client is caught between conflicting desires, and needs to resolve the issue if he is to grow. By means of a psychodramatic technique, his struggle is intensified and an impasse occurs.

C. What I want to work with is my old feelings of not meeting expectations, therefore, feeling like the other person doesn't love me—is rejecting me—because I'm not doing what I think they want me to do. However, I feel I am more in control than where I was. I am letting my own feelings show. It feels good too. There is a point that I block; I can have so much; can't have too much. (Chuckles) Too much of a good thing you know. Not ready for that yet. (Joking)

M. I see a smile on your face, sort of a half-smile. What's happening?

C. I feel good, and still I feel a polarity. (Polarity now becomes my focus.)

M. What are the two sides?

C. I feel very warm towards people and I can feel very cold towards people.

M. How about having two people play the polarities?

C. Okay (He chooses two group members.) Betty, you are the cold part. You are tense and you are cold. You are facing me. Sort of hunched over.

M. Have her say a typical word or sentence characterizing you. (It is important that words be selected *by the client* rather than improvised by others.)

C. "I'm cold."

M. Okay, now your positive side? (He selects a group member, Alan, and asks him to say "I'm open.") All right, I would like you two (i.e., his polarities) to say your lines repeatedly. (To C) Do whatever you want; pay attention to them, deal with them. (The scene is now set. As the two polarities bombard him with their respective positions, he will feel the increasing pressure.)

A. "I'm open."

B. "I'm cold."

(The voices continue unabated.)

C. I want to be open. I'm wanting more openness than what I am. I am blocking her out. I hear her, but I don't even look at her.

M. Are you saying she'll go away if you don't pay any attention to her? (He thinks that by ignoring or blocking out a part of his personality, that part will "go away.")

C. Yes.

M. Try it and see what happens.

(The "voices" continue.)

C. She's not going away. I want her to go away. (Laughs)

(The "voices" continue unabated.)

M. I don't think she is going to go away by wishing her gone or pretending she is not there. I suggest an entirely different approach. Thank her and tell her your appreciation for all that she has done for you. (Character defenses are formed in childhood as a response to life stresses. The defense represents the child's best available coping mechanism. Although the defense mechanism may be archaic, nevertheless it deserves appreciation for services rendered.)

C. Oh shit! (Sighs)

M. She may have been a friend and perhaps is no longer needed.

C. Yeah.

M. I imagine you are feeling some uncomfortableness.

C. YEAH, very much.

M. Perhaps you don't want to show your appreciation for that part. (The client resists, being in touch only with the negative aspects of his character trait.)

C. After what she's done to me.

M. *For* you . . . not *to* you.

B. "I'm cold! I'm cold! I'm cold!"

C. (To Betty) "Shut up. (Laughs) I appreciate you (Laughs again) because you covered up my fear. You covered up my fear for quite a few years now. (Long silence) You helped me escape from things that I didn't want to face. I appreciate the purpose that you served."

M. Do you want to dismiss her, say good-bye, or keep her in reserve for some future time?

C. (Laughs) "I don't need you anymore. I am glad to get rid of you. I feel that I am rid of you now."

M. You look good. You look beaming.

C. I am feeling better, I can function. (Laughs) It's too much of a good thing. (Laughs) Don't get too much of a good thing.

M. I appreciated you really being able to thank her sincerely for what she'd done for you as part of your survival rather than your saying "get out," being ungrateful.

C. I needed her.

Only by accepting what *is*, i.e., reality, can alternative choices be considered. What "could" be, "should" be, "might" be, etc., are illusions. This client has accepted a previously disowned and disliked element and therefore no longer invests energy in repressing and blocking part of himself.

EXORCISING THE FATHER

This work commences in the "classic" gestalt manner. The client begins with a top dog/underdog conflict. An impasse occurs, since neither "dog" can win.

J. I feel dead, tense, constricted. I don't like it. I want to be spontaneous. My face feels dead. My cheeks don't move. My eyes don't move and I don't like it. I want to fight it; I want to make it different.

M. The more you fight, the less you are going to accomplish. (Perls said that the way to gain control is to lose control.)

J. I've read that in books and I don't know how to do it.

M. I would like you to do the opposite. *Be* all those symptoms that you have. (Increasing his awareness of his "symptoms" by means of exaggeration.)

J. (Long silence) I'm dead, (Pause) I'm stonefaced, not even looking anywhere. I'm just sitting here. Oblivious to anything here. There is tension in my neck.

M. Are there any images or fantasies that go along with your deadness?

J. (Long silence) Yes. I want others to like me. I want those people over there to like me. Unless I listen to them completely, unless I'm with them they won't like me. I don't want to be with them. I want to be with me. (A preliminary and still intellectual insight)

M. Okay. Be with you.

J. My neck is looser now. (Pause)

M. I have a hunch that you have an awful lot of *shoulds* operating. Is that true?

J. Yes.

M. Would you pick someone to play your "should" voice. (He picks a group member, Lenny.) Where do you want your "should" voice to be?

J. Right over my shoulder. I want him up here. Kind of down at me. Deep, strong, powerful, accusatory.

M. Give him some sample lines. (The words used are very important and should be selected by the client. This is in contrast to a psychodrama, where participants will improvise their parts. In my opinion, the improvisations tend to dilute the intensity of the experience.)

J. "You should work harder. You should do more. You should see more people. Be more tuned in. Forget yourself. Don't think about yourself. You should work hard."

M. What's the other side? Is there a part of you that says "relax?" (Since there is a top dog, I assume there is an underdog.)

J. Yeah, it's a little bitty thing. Kathie would you play it? You are weak and you can just barely whisper. That's about all you can do.

M. Give her some lines.

J. (In a low voice) "I want to dance. I want to give the finger to somebody. I wanna say I'm bored."

L. "You should work harder. You should do more!"

K. "I want to dance."

L. "You should try harder. You should do better. You should be looser."

K. "Oh, fuck it." (Low voice)

L. "You should be friendlier. You should be better. You should work harder.

K. "I wanna have some fun."

L. "You should try harder. You should be a better person."

K. "I wanna go out someplace."

L. "You should be nice to people."

J. SHUT UP! (Screams) (He is finally getting angry.)

L. "You should be nice . . ."

J. (Screams) LEAVE ME ALONE!

K. "I want to be nasty to people."

L. "You should be nice to people. You should be nice to people."

K. "I wanna give you the finger."

L. "You should be nice to people."

K. "Fuck it!"

L. "You should hold your temper. You should be calmer."

K. "I don't wanna be calm."

L. "Be in control."

K. "I don't want to be in control."

L. "You should keep your feelings in."

K. "I don't want to."

L. "You shouldn't have fun."

K. "I wanna have fun."

L. "You should do more. You should keep doing what . . ."

J. DAMN IT, LEAVE ME ALONE. WILL YOU SHUT UP? (Screams this)

L. "Do more!"

J. NO, NO, NO!

L. "You should do more. You should do more."

J. I don't have to!

L. "You should do more!"

J. I'll do what I want! (Angry) (He is finally becoming assertive.)

L. "You should work harder. You should be better!"

J. Now that I am here, I don't know what to do now. I feel like I'm not at either one of those.

M. You're at the impasse. Stay with it and see what you decide to do. (The struggle between his top dog and underdog resumes.)

J. "Dad, look you've worked hard all your life and I've worked the way you did." (He has never mentioned Dad thus far. Apparently Dad is his top dog. At this point he is separating his existence from his father's.)

L. "You should keep working."

J. "I wanna have some fun."

L. "You shouldn't have fun."

J. "You've worked hard all your life and that was best for you. But, that's not always best for me. Now would you just let me alone! Let me run my own life the way I want to."

L. "You should keep working."

J. "I do! I do. I'll do my best. But then, that's enough. Let me have it my own way . . . and have some time for me."

M. "You're not me." Say that a few times.

J. "You're not me. You're not me. You're not me. You're my father. And you are a good man. You're fine your way, but you are not me. I'm OK this way. I don't have to be a little you. You've wanted me to for all my life, but I can't do that. I've worked hard as hell for twenty-six fuckin' years to do that. Get off my back and let me alone. (Voice angry) I can do things myself and I don't need you to tell me what to do!"

M. Before stopping, make contact with a few people starting your statements with "I'm Jack." Be any way that you want to be at that moment. Don't stop and think about it. (Giving him the experience of integrating and solidifying his identity. My request not to pause and think is to encourage him to be spontaneous. This work represents the beginnings, not the conclusions, of his striving for identity.)

Chapter V

SPECIFIC APPLICATIONS

WORKING WITH PROBLEM DRINKERS WHO DO NOT WANT TO STOP DRINKING: A GESTALT AWARENESS PROCESS*

Paul E. Paige, M.S.W.

In the last decade, I have had the good fortune to work with over 3,000 people who were seriously involved in alcohol abuse. Within this spectrum were included simple excessive drinkers, problem drinkers (alpha alcoholics), people who manifested physical dependency and were out of control in their drinking (gamma alcoholics), episodic drinkers who went on binges (epsilon alcoholics), as well as the neurologically damaged and Koraskoff syndrome patients. This experience has been in a variety of settings: private outpatient clinics, private hospitals, county hospitals, state hospitals, skid row, recovery homes, legal justice system, and private practice. In working with abusers of alcohol and other drugs, in a variety of settings, my experience has been more successful than not; and as a result, I continue to pursue this area of investigation and intervention. I want to share a clinical perspective that has evolved in my work with alcohol abusers who say they do not want to stop drinking.

An enduring question that is always present with every good clinician is: How do we effect successful treatment of those people who did not respond to whatever approach had been used in the past? After hundreds of therapeutic "postmortems" with people

---

*A version of this paper has been published in *VOICES*, Spring edition, 1975.

who have been unsuccessfully treated by a variety of clinicians, one central conclusion emerges. The clinicians' closing remarks usually include statements to the effect that: (1) the patient does not want to stop drinking; (2) the patient has a ways to go yet before he hits bottom and is ready to change; (3) the patient is not serious and does not have enough motivation. These comments may in fact be true, and/or they may be explanations for clinical and therapeutic failure on the part of the professional therapist or counselor. I believe the latter is more true in most cases that are unsucessfully treated.

Recently, in reviewing about 1,000 case histories of people who had deteriorated enough to be hospitalized in Camarillo State Hospital in California, the most outstanding feature was that all of the people had received treatment at least twice before being sent there. All had been hospitalized at least once before and had tried to utilize at least two community rehabilitation resources: physicians, Alcoholics Anonymous, outpatient clinics, or medical hospitals. These patients consistently reported having actively attempted to utilize at least three of these resources at different points in their drinking career, and consistently reported little or no success.

These patients reported that they felt "motivated" in at least two of their "sincere" attempts at obtaining help early in their drinking career, before they had lost everything; *but* they had not been able to stop drinking or could not maintain their sobriety long enough. A surprising finding, in reviewing this case history material, was that all of the patients had had significant periods of sobriety within the year prior to admission to the hospital and had not had continuous drinking. Also, nearly all reported extended periods of sobriety (nearly six months) within the last five years. All of them had been able to stop drinking and did. This was surprising, since most of these people reported that they were not able to stop drinking. They had in fact stopped. Yet they started again.

This distinction is important, that there was not continuous drinking. Evidently, the period of abstinence was not satisfying and complete enough for them. There was something vital and important missing in their lives, and in the way they were attempting to straighten themselves out. Sobriety in and of itself was not enough.

FACTORS IN UNCONTROLLED DRINKING

Individuals who are experiencing difficulty through problem drinking and refuse to stop, regardless of environmental and personal pressures, suffer from a lack of ego strength. Ego strength is defined here as the ability to identify with one's emotional and body state, ability to control impulses and direct functioning into appropriate reality tasks. High ego strength has been related to successful treatment in psychotherapy and is used as a prognostic factor in determining outcome of treatment. A simple formulation is possible: ego strength is necessary for self-control.

Usually what lies behind the problem drinker's reluctance to stop drinking is:

1. He has inadequate resources to deal with internal distress and disorganization.
2. He experiences a lack of alternates to drinking as a coping mechanism.
3. He has an inability to feel what is going on in his body, as a result of the anesthetic effects of alcohol and proprioceptive anesthetic (he is cut off and has "lost the feel" of himself).
4. He is still achieving positive benefits through the use of alcohol.
5. He is maintaining the illusion that he is a "happy drunk" most of the time.
6. He has a basic fear that he will not be able to stop even if he tries as hard as possible.

The last item, basic fear that he will not be able to stop even if he puts everything into it, is the central issue of concern. When a change agent (doctor, minister, court, therapeutic counselor) is able to get a "commitment" or promise from the patient to "try" to stop all drinking immediately, both the therapist and the patient are forced into an impasse, and the patient does not have the ego strength or the resources to face or go through such an impasse. The patient retreats, feeling less than he did before, more inadequate and more convinced that he is not able to control himself or sustain positive action on his own behalf. An all-or-nothing imperative sets him up for another failure that further damages his ego and depletes what motivation he may have. At this point he may lose confidence in his ability to mount an effort on his own behalf, and he may lose confidence in the professional he is working with to know him and his capabilities.

I have seen doctors, therapists, and counselors set up an all-or-nothing ultimatum; when the patient fails to meet the therapist's expectations, he is admonished for his lack of sincerity or seriousness. The patient will usually fade into the distance and disappear, or will come back again to get beaten over the head with his inability to control himself, *which is his basis for seeking professional advice.* The key is that the person does not know *how.* Doctors and other professionals tell the person *what* to do and do not work with how to accomplish it. This is the area of gestalt therapy, the what and how in the here and now. Working centrally with the what and how is necessary and sufficient to effect stabilization.

A major axiom that constantly emerges is: If the patient is not in treatment, you cannot treat him. The converse is true also; as long as he is involved in treatment, then treatment is possible.

De facto with the person's being in treatment, he is wanting something and is willing to invest his time, money, and whatever little else is available at that moment. This "whatever little else" that is available may not be enough to accomplish anastrophic results like cessation of all drinking immediately; however, whatever is there is enough for a humanistic counselor to start working with. As a matter of fact, what is at that moment, with that person, is all there is to work with. It does not really matter how little or meager the resources the person is presenting; he is there, concerned, wanting, and in my opinion workable. The basic approach is to start where the client is, not where we would like him to be. Take him seriously and begin a systematic approach to engage him in treatment, sustain and maintain his motivation, build his ego strength and his knowledge bases, and begin to increase his alternates to the use of alcohol. As long as the person is coming in and is there, he is workable. A professional need not throw him away because he did not meet specific expectations. To do so makes the therapist no different from other lay people who have done the same.

DIFFERENT TYPES OF PROBLEM DRINKERS

In general practice we usually see three types of problem drinkers:

1. The person who has a serious problem with alcohol, where substance abuse is seriously interfering with one of the major life processes and the person does not recognize or accept that alcohol is the problem.
2. The person who acknowledges that alcohol is a problem and freely admits that he *has* to stop, wants to stop, and thinks he is not able.
3. The person who intellectually admits that alcohol creates problems of health, employment, and relationships, and legal problems, and says he does not want to stop drinking.

I work in several ways with these different types of problem drinkers, depending on who they are, the resources available, and the best possible way to effect intervention, based on their reality and the way they present themselves to be worked with. The possible modes of intervention and goals are:

1. Working directly with the person, directly on their drinking; goal is no drinking or other drug abuse (legal or illegal).
2. Working directly with the person, indirectly on their drinking; goal is no drinking or drug abuse.

3. Working directly with the person, directly on their drinking; goal is limited and controlled drinking.

4. Working directly with the person, indirectly on their drinking; goal is limited and controlled drinking.

5. Working indirectly with the person (working with a wife, child, relative, or close friend) directly on drinking; goal is self-adjustment of the person that I'm working with, helping them to become a real resource for helping the problem drinker.

6. Working with a spouse, child, relative, or friend, indirectly on drinking; goal is self-adjustment of the person that I'm working with, exploring what is possible in the affected relationship, and controlled or no drinking.

The type of problem drinker who says that he does not want to stop drinking is always the most difficult and frustrating type of person to work with and is the subject of this paper. Frequently we see the waste of human resource and potential of people who have a serious problem, who do not want to stop drinking, who freely admit that they like drinking and still get a lot from it. The situation is usually complex, with one or several coercive agents pressuring the person to cease drinking altogether:

1. Mandate from physician that the person will not live long
2. Ultimatum by spouse that they will leave or kick the problem drinker out
3. Ultimatum by boss that employment will be curtailed-ended
4. Ultimatum by legal authorities involving suspension of license or jail

It is important to understand the background of this person in order to treat him. The patient has been manipulated and coerced into treatment to change behavior that he really does not want to change. The person has had subtle and obvious pressures applied and has been threatened by the most important people in his life; yet his drinking behavior has not changed, and may have in many cases worsened.

The person has presented wishful thinking and promises like, "I'm going to stop drinking," and yet he persists in his drinking behavior. The person in effect is being sent to a counselor or doctor to be further manipulated, or to be changed by a professional change agent. In my experience as a counselor and psychotherapist, I have not been able to get anyone to do what they did not want to do. I have learned this lesson over and over again. Ultimately, people do exactly what they are willing to do. If the professional accepts the task of mandating that the person stop drinking completely, he then becomes a part of the alcoholic game of "Bet you can't stop me." If the therapist is a skillful manipulator and if the patient's cost of drinking is high, there may be brief periods of sobriety and abstinence, but there will also be both brief and protracted drinking bouts, and the counselor will always wind up defeated, feeling frustrated and used.

Siding with a person's resistances and changing personality resistance into personality assistance has been implicit throughout the evolution of gestalt therapy. Arnold Beisser (1970) has conceptualized this as the Theory of Paradoxical Change: "Change occurs when one becomes what he is, not when he tries to become what he is not." Change does not take place through a coercive attempt by the individual, or by another person, to change him. It does take place if the individual takes the time and effort to be what he is—to be fully invested in his current position. When the professional rejects the role of change agent, he makes meaningful and orderly change possible.

This feeling of being frustrated and used is common to most people in the helping professions and is the basis of their refusal to work with these types of patients. It is my opinion that professionals who have these experiences have set themselves up for it by siding with the coerceive agents, becoming an extension of the person's conflict as he asks the patient to do the impossible (patient's view): completely stop drinking. This is what Fritz Perls (1973) has called a topdog/underdog struggle, with the change agent winding up as the topdog.

What I am suggesting is that the counselor side with the person's resistance and work within that framework on the side of the patient, and help him learn to use himself instead of abuse himself and alcohol. When a professional sides with the resistance and is willing to work with what is, he will discover that personality resistance will change into assistance and that the patient will trust him and be willing to explore new ways of seeing and being in the world. Otherwise, the professional becomes only one more coercive agent, crystallizing the person's resistance and his stubbornness by demanding that the patient stop drinking immediately. Mark and Linda Sobell (1972) have pointed out that in some cases, during acute drinking, insistence upon abstinence as the *only* possible treatment goal may be unrealistic or harmful. The person may try his best to abstain from all drinking and find that he is unable to tolerate the *immediate* consequences of not being intoxicated and not having this coping mechanism available to him. What results is another failure and collapse of inspiration and motivation to do something about himself and his problem. In spite of the consequences, the person continues to ingest large amounts of alcohol and continues to perpetuate or worsen his condition. The Sobells point out that the issue here is not the morality of the consequences, but rather the reality of the person involved in the consequences.

The alcohol-abusing person who does not want to stop really knows that he is hurting himself; however, at this point in his life, he is not able to face that hurt and pain by himself. His reality is that he does not have any better alternate that he knows and trusts will work for him. He is faced with an impasse: stop using and abusing and do what? Additionally, he does not have the basic trust and faith in himself or the professional he is working with to go through the impasse. The patient's impasse soon becomes the practitioner's dilemma: The patient has to stop drinking or he is not going to get better, and I cannot help him.

AN AWARENESS PROCESS

An alternate to the dilemma of abstinence or rejection is what I call a controlled drinking schedule. I develop a contract with the patient to bring his drinking under control and begin dealing with the consequences in a realistic, step-by-step fashion. By controlled drinking I mean "a specified amount, at a specified time, under specified conditions, with an explicit contract agreed upon and freely entered into by both parties, the counselor and the patient."

In most cases, the person is not fully aware of how much he is currently drinking. He may know that he is drinking too much but not be fully cognizant of what that really means.

The *First Step* is for the counselor to go over the previous week with the patient to establish a good estimate of the quality, quantity, circumstances, and financial cost of the drinking behavior. This will establish a baseline to work from and give the counselor an idea of the depth of the problem.

The *Second Step* is to have the person keep an accurate record at the end of each evening of the day's drinking, the quality, quantity, circumstances, with whom, and the cost. This method will bring into the patient's awareness exactly what he is doing. The record will give the counselor some idea of how motivated the patient is and how well he can follow directions.

The *Third Step* consists of a study of the structure and function of the drinking behavior. The counselor pays attention to details and finds out what the different parts of drinking mean to the person, before trying to deal with the whole. Find out what parts the person likes, what parts he gets something from, and what parts he does not like and from which he gets negative benefits.

The *Fourth Step* is that the counselor and patient mutually compile a complete and detailed record of every use of alcohol, detailing the "solutions" that alcohol is providing for the problems being coped with, exploring and specifying alternates that are mutually acceptable.

The *Fifth Step* is the developing and detailing by the counselor of the therapeutic work necessary to develop functional and creative alternates to some of the real problems the person is facing, such as handling anger, anxiety, and awkwardness.

The *Sixth Step* is when the person is fully aware of the extent of the use and abuse of alcohol and specific areas are targeted to "work through" therapeutically. Concomitantly, there is a cessation of the use of alcohol as a means of coping, when the function of the use is no longer needed. The person no longer needs to rely on alcohol as a means, but can use his own resources and be free to choose what he wants to do, including to use or abuse himself.

When a person becomes aware of the structure and function of his drinking, it begins to change immediately. From the focus on drinking, the counselor begins to expand awareness with the person of himself and the world. The problem drinker begins to learn-discover possibilities for his own growth and development and to generate his own creative adjustment instead of using alcohol or other drugs to cope with the world and himself.

PHASES IN THE TREATMENT PROCESS

The patient will go through three basic phases, which are typical of all alcohol-abuse patients, drug-abuse patients, and some other patients in treatment: STABILITY, RECOVERY, DISCOVERY. In order to discuss the stage of stability, which is the focus here, I will first define the other two stages*:

Recovery is where the person focuses on recovering the disowned parts of himself that are central to his existence and full functioning. Frequently this is "typical" Gestalt work as seen in general practice with *over-controlled* patients. In order for the person to stop drinking and elevate himself from an *uncontrolled* drinking posture, he has exaggerated to an extreme his hold on himself, and he has lost the ability to feel fully, live deeply, and extend himself to other people and the outside world, and so he needs to recover his fluidity and expressivity.

Discovery is the final process whereby a person is stabilized, has ceased most toxic behavior, including drinking, and has recovered personality functions and abilities. The motivational process

*For further discussion, see Paige, 1972.

progresses from (1) "DESPERATION" to obtain stability; to (2) "INSPIRATION" to recover feelings and full function; to (3) "FASCINATION" to discover what is really possible in his life. The discovery process is where a person will want and be able to expand his life and expressive functions and develop a creative life-style. Working on the "adjustment strategy of therapy," getting the person to adjust to his banal existence is antithetical to this life process. This is the point of maximum growth and development where a person can best integrate advanced experiences and techniques such as Rolfing and other in-depth and expansive forms of growth. At this juncture, the drive for new experiences, in order to expand personal fulfillment, is completely internal and self-directed. The role of the professional radically changes to a fellow pedestrian in the pursuit of alternate ways of seeing and being in the world.

Stability, the first phase in the treatment process, is a process which has three major sequences that are reasonably predictable:

1. **Initial Euphoria.** The person discovers that he has broken the cycle of progressive drinking, that he can control his drinking, and that he is not "out of control." He will begin to feel better physically and emotionally, and his environment (job, spouse, friends, and therapist) will provide positive feedback that the person looks better and is behaving better and that things are better. However, this sequence and the person's enthusiasm are usually short-lived.
2. **Transitional Crises.** The changes that occur usually create an imbalance and precipitate one of several crises, either from a spouse/spouse-surrogate (see Paige, Le Pointe, & Krueger, 1971) or from the environment (job, friends, the law, or debts). The patient may attempt to solve these crises by his habitual response, an increase in alcohol consumption. It is very important that the professional not reject the person for doing what is second nature to him, but rather work through the sequences of the drinking episodes and use this situation as a learning experience to explore and develop precise alternates that the person may have developed

and can use in the future, instead of alcohol. Not only does the coping mechanism (drinking) need to be worked with, but the actual crises need to be dealt with, such as handling a spouse who is playing uproar and attempting (inadvertently or intentionally) to sabotage the treatment process.

3. **Grounding.** This is a bioenergetic concept that is fully described by Stanley Keleman (1973): "To me grounding means being anchored in our physical-psychic growth process: expanding, contracting (contract and withdrawal), charging and discharging." The opposite of grounding is flight, or interference with our human essence or substance, which results in fear, rage, frustration, and dissatisfaction. People who use drugs interfere with their biological bases of orientation and are spaced out of their own organisms. Grounding is the most important sequence in the stabilization process, where the person regains some of his ability to feel himself and becomes oriented in his own body and psyche. Grounding is an ongoing process and continues through the treatment process, with the person becoming more and more settled and feeling at home in his own skin. A related process is centering, which functions during the stabilization process. Centering is a concept used by many gestalt therapists to describe where the essence of activity, influence, and power are experienced by any person. Alcohol and other drug abusers experience their "center" outside of themselves, which may be in a substance, in a particular relationship, or in the outside world in general. When a person is centered, he is responsive and response-able, to himself and his environment, and the essence of action emanates from within him.

When a person has become stabilized and connected with the professional he is working with, he is settled in the therapeutic relationship. He has confidence in the person that he is working with and confidence in himself. He begins to believe that he and his life can be better, and he does have the resources to be effective with his own problems. He believes that he realistically does have the power (ego strength) to change himself and his circumstances, when he learns to use himself instead of alcohol. He believes that he is acceptable as a person to the professional and views that professional as an ally or as a personal consultant, and believes the professional is not going to disregard him or attempt to manipulate or coerce him.

When the patient has become connected in the therapeutic relationship, he will begin to rely on, use, and trust the therapist. By establishing bases of understanding and mutual respect, acceptance and trust with the counselor, the person then becomes able to accept, trust, and understand himself. The person at this point in concluding the stabilization process is enjoying his sobriety and feels that he is substantial and real. This is the point at which most hospitalized patients would be discharged, as they look good and report feeling good. Unless treatment is continued into the next phase, recovery, this stability will be limited and short-lived, and the person will later decompensate.

This stabilization process provides the sustenance and fiber necessary to do the real therapeutic work of successfully working through the chronic depression and underlying neurosis. The real therapeutic work involves a greater amount of investment, risk taking, and ego strength in order to recover the disowned parts of one's personality and move toward integration and wholeness. The stability phase of treatment has provided the person with solid ground on which to stand on his own two feet and to improve his standing in the world, without the use or abuse of alcohol or other drugs.

SUMMARY

A clinical attitude on the part of the professional is described, which when adopted, can make the therapeutic work possible. This clinical perspective is not unique to gestalt therapy, or a humanistic framework; however it does afford the most congruence from that perspective. The process outlined could be taken in conjunction with many different therapies—with different results.

In general practice we see three types of alcohol abusers: (1) the alcohol abuser who does not accept that alcohol is a problem; (2) the alcohol abuser who freely admits that alcohol is a problem and that he has to stop, and (3) the alcohol abuser who intellectually admits that alcohol creates problems of health, employment, etc., and he refuses to stop drinking. A clinical approach to working with this resistance is recommended in which the professional does not side with the coercive agents; rather, engages the person in treatment and sides with his resistance, in order to get the person stabilized, so the real problems the person is having difficulty with can be successfully treated. Alcohol, as such, is not the problem. Rather, it has functioned as a "solution" to a variety of problems these people have faced.

REFERENCES

Beisser, A.R. The paradoxical theory of change. In: Fagen, J. and Shepherd, I.L. eds. Gestalt Therapy Now. Palo Alto, Science and Behavior Books, 1970.

Keleman, S. The Human Ground. San Francisco, Lodestar Press, 1973.

Paige, P.E. A Humanistic treatment program for the treatment of the substance abuser. Monograph. Santa Monica, P. Paige & Associates, 1972.

Paige, P.E., La Pointe, W. and Krueger, A. The marital dyad as a diagnostic and treatment variable in alcohol addiction. Psychology, 8, 64-74, 1971.

Perls, F. The gestalt approach & eye witness to therapy. Palo Alto, Science and Behavior Books, 1973.

Sobell, M. and Sobell, L. Individualized behavior therapy for alcoholics. Research Monograph, California Department of Mental Hygiene, 1972.

GESTALT THERAPY WITH CHILDREN—HOW IT COMPARES WITH GESTALT THERAPY WITH ADULTS

Charles S. Brudo, Ph.D.

INTRODUCTION

It is assumed that the reader of this chapter already understands what Gestalt Therapy itself is about. This chapter aims to consider, from the view of the Gestalt therapist, the differences between working with children and working with adults.

Gestalt therapy was evolved by Dr. Fritz Perls from his professional lifetime of experience in working with adults, but not with children. In effect, his theories of personality and psychotherapy and his training procedures were addressed only to adults. Similarly, his colleague and former student, James S. Simkin, while developing his own style, techniques, and theoretical considerations, was principally involved with adults.

When, in the middle of the 1960s, I started my training in Gestalt Therapy with Perls and Simkin, I had had more than ten years' experience in working therapeutically with both children and adults. At that time nothing had been published concerning Gestalt Therapy with children, nor did Gestalt Therapy training even allude to children.

Since then a few writings about Gestalt work with children have been published. Cohn (1970) has written about her Gestalt-Psychoanalytic work with one child. Kempler (1973) has discussed and demonstrated some Gestalt principles in action in his work with children in family therapy. Lederman (1970) has written of her Gestalt work with young children within a school setting. Rhyne (1973) has written about the use of art in Gestalt therapy both with children and with adults. I would like to add to this information by reporting some of my salient impressions, experiences, and conclusions regarding what I have found as a Gestalt therapist in working with children.

Before going into some detail, I want to state that I have found that working with children does involve special considerations. I have also found that some of the Gestalt techniques developed with adults (e.g., Perls's work with dreams) can readily be used with children. And that most of the techniques already used by child therapists of various orientations lend themselves especially well to mediating the therapeutic interaction which ensues from the Gestalt Therapy view of the ongoing life process.

THREE MAJOR FACTORS WHICH ARE IMPLICIT IN WORKING WITH CHILDREN, AND WHICH DO MAKE A DIFFERENCE AS COMPARED WITH GESTALT WORK WITH ADULTS

In my work with children, three major factors have emerged which for me make for appreciable difference in the modes of applicability of Gestalt Therapy. These three factors are:

1. The fact that children do not live through words as much as adults do.
2. The fact that children usually come into therapy at their parents' initiative—not their own.
3. The reality of child dependency on the parents or parent surrogates.

None of these factors is new. The therapists who work with children take them as self-evident. However, as I attempted to transfer my Gestalt training experience from adults to children, these factors acquired renewed vividness.

1. I have stated that children do not live through words as much as adults do. While the proportion of children who are verbally fluent may be as great as the proportion of adults who are, children more than adults express themselves and experience themselves in action, in play, in acting out their fantasies (hence the use of play therapy with children). This, of course, is *advantageous* for Gestalt therapists, as Gestalt Therapy *does emphasize* experiencing through sensory and motor involvement—action—rather than through words alone. However, the fact remains that even Gestalt Therapy relies heavily on words as a medium of experience. For instance, the continuum of awareness process, the top-dog/underdog and "give a voice to" techniques require words as a medium for attaining and expressing experience of oneself. The various scripts in Perls's *Gestalt Therapy Verbatim* (1969) and other Gestalt texts bear out this fact.

Furthermore, while there is a marked difference between adults and children in how much they express and experience through action rather than words, there is also a major qualitative difference as to how children and adults use words. Children much more than adults express themselves symbolically. While playing out fantasies they may be soldiers, or mothers, or Superman, or animals, or babies, or fathers, or baseball stars, or robbers, or pilots.

Another factor that applies particularly to children is that of the apparently painful association connected with direct verbal interaction with adults. I find that some children frequently resist expressing their feelings directly in a verbal way. I am not referring to a developmental maturational phenomenon, nor to the skill that children do or do not have with words, nor to their usual reliance on action rather than words for expression. I am referring to *resistance*, to *avoidance*. Most child therapists have faced the reality of some children's reluctance, avoidance, resistance to "talking."

From the context of my clinical experience with children and their families, I have hypothesized that these children have acutely experienced verbal interaction as a means used by adults to manipulate them, or to belittle them, or to make demands upon them that they can't or don't wish to satisfy. Or, these children have frequently experienced being smothered under an avalanche of words from parents or surrogate parents. Serious, direct verbal interaction with adults has been painful to them and they avoid it. In other instances, children have introjected the injunction, "You are not to say to me things which oppose my views or my actions, or which are hostile to me."

Whatever the circumstances attendant to the development of such resistance to talking, one could say that it would be therapeutic to offer the child opportunities to gain or to acquire the power to talk meaningfully about himself. Yes, it would be. However, at the time of initial contact other problems might be much more in the foreground, much more meaningful to the child than his unwillingness or undeveloped ability to speak. The Gestalt therapist, putting first things first, would therefore address himself to the foreground problems without first having to be involved with the matter of verbalizing.

2. The second difference I have mentioned is that children are more frequently than not brought to the therapist at the parents' initiative, rather than at their own. Perls states (1973, pp. 110-11) that

> Gestalt therapy makes the basic assumption that the patient is lacking in self-support, and that the therapist symbolizes the patient's incomplete self. The first step in therapy then is to find out what the patient needs. If he is not psychotic . . . the patient is partly aware of his needs and can at least partially express them. But there are some areas in which the patient is either unaware of his specific needs, or is blocked in demanding what he wants. Often the therapist finds that the patient is ashamed to make certain requests, equally often he finds that the patient is convinced that the only valuable help he can get is help that is guessed and given without being asked for. Often he does not know how to ask, or he is confused about what he really

> wants. But once he can express his demands, his orders, his commands and his requests directly and actually mean what he says, he has made the most important step in all of his therapy.

The fact is, however, that a child may or may not know what a therapist is. So that he may know even less what he wants from the therapist. However, he might know what he wants, not in reference to the therapist, but in reference to his life. He wants his mother to stop nagging him, or his father to stop losing his temper, or he wants to stop having nightmares, or he would like other children to like him. Or a child may be so little in touch with himself that he may not be aware of any wants—everything is fine. And if he has a dim awareness of some wants he may feel too great a taboo on expressing his wants. Other children may, with various degrees of accuracy, experience their being brought to a therapist as a reflection of their parents' dissatisfaction with them, or with themselves, or both. This experience often is saliently in the foreground and overshadows the pains, frustrations, or anger they may have in other areas.

Hence the gestalt therapist working with children will often find much more frequently than with adults that the child is unclear as to what he wants, or that what he wants is to *not* be brought to a therapist, or that he has strongly ambivalent feelings about it. Working with what is in the foreground for the child, and in the context of the background, the Gestalt therapist will stay with the foreground and thereby establish and maintain contact, and interact with the child. Thus, with the therapist staying with the child, the child will frequently, but not always, accept the therapist as a means of furthering his self-realization.

On occasion the child will continue to reject the therapist's services regardless of how well the therapist stays with the child. For instance, the child might so strongly feel that accepting the therapist would be, in effect, agreeing with his parents' overt or implied belief that the child and the child only is "the one who needs changing," that he staunchly and persistently refuses to accept the therapeutic services—especially so when the parents themselves are not, at that point, willing to deviate from their position.

This refusal sometimes underlies a talking avoidance not yet mentioned. While some children verbalize their refusal, some express it by avoiding talking about the issues presented by the parents, and some by hardly talking at all. While a child may feel and be powerless in regard to being brought to the therapist, he finds himself quite able to refuse to interact with the therapist. Refusing to interact, then, is the form of interaction that the therapist would likely address himself to. And this brings us to the third factor I wanted to mention.

3. In reference to this third factor, I want to note that throughout his writings Fritz Perls emphasizes the importance of the growth of the patient's attitude of self-support—his response-ability (responsibility). This is a major process which contributes to the dissolution of "neurotic," non-self-realizing attitudes. It appears that for most adults in our culture this is a possible and realizable way of functioning.

As Perls states, the adult is not self-sufficient. He does depend on others for survival and for gratification. But, as Perls emphasizes, to the extent that a person does support his self—to the extent he has self-support—to this extent he is free to use his energies to provide for himself in those areas where he is not self-sufficient. In reference to children, however, their extreme lack of self-sufficiency, their extreme dependence on others for survival, are of paramount importance in the development or lack of development of self-support. Hence it is imperative that the child's parents or parent-surrogates be involved in the therapeutic process.

Fritz Perls and Gestalt therapists in general usually refrain from "helping" the patient directly, as this in effect often reinforces the neurotic patterns already present. They focus instead on creating a milieu of circumstances that permit self-realization. However, the younger the child the greater his actual dependency on a given set of adults: his parents. Sometimes the child has parents or parent-surrogates who, through their own emotional dysfunction, in effect demand that the child become subdued and dependent and remain so. In such circumstances, and in spite of the therapist's efforts, the child may not be able to develop much autonomy. The child may sense consciously or unconsciously, but often with a certain degree of realism, that his survival as an emotional and physical entity may depend on sacrificing, deadening, various aspects of himself including his self-support. Joen Fagan (1974, p. 4) well expressed this point in reference to doing therapy with schizophrenic adults:

> In long-term therapy with schizophrenics—a confusing and frustrating process—it's helped my sanity at times to see that I'm dealing with two children in a room: an infant and a five year old. The infant is hungry, wet, cold and crying. There are footsteps in the hall; an adult-parent is walking by and about to come in. The five-year old knows that if the parent hears the infant crying, she'll kill him, so he begins all kinds of noise-making, attention-directing, distracting, denying behavior. It works, and the parent doesn't hear that crying infant and leaves. The five-year old then turns to the infant, and cares for him as best he can, considering that he doesn't have enough muscle to pick him up, and that he has only crackers for food and paper towels for diapers.
>
> In T.A. terms, this impasse is between the little Adult in the Child and the Child in the Child . . . . The parental injunction from the Child of the mother to the to-be-schizophrenic infant is "Don't Need," which, for an infant, is almost identical to "Don't Be," but comes more from the helplessness of the mother than from her anger. Since the needs of the infant for nurturing, closeness, etc. cause in the mother very powerful anxiety and self-doubts, the premature little Adult develops to understand the mother and to supress the infant's needs in order to keep the mother from deserting completely or becoming furious and killing him.

Here is another respect in which the gestalt therapist trained with adults finds his work somewhat different: Whereas the adults he has worked with have usually had some motivation to seek therapy for themselves, the parents of troubled children frequently are not aware that they themselves are likely to be very much part of their child's problems. This lack of awareness may be a reflection of their psychological naivete or a concomitant of their self-alienation. Sometimes the parents' statements of what they want involves the assertion, "I have nothing to do with the way Johnny is," and the demand, "Change him." The gestalt therapist working with children must be willing to relate therapeutically with reluctant parents, and besides doing therapy with them, must be willing to educate and inform them.

In the example which follows, the therapist erroneously assumed that the dramatic presenting symptoms that the child and mother described were in the foreground, and overlooked the likelihood that therapy could not proceed satisfactorily without immediately focusing on the mother as well as on the child. In the occasion I have in mind, an eleven-year-old boy was in great emotional pain. His mother was in a gestalt therapy group but had only had three or four sessions. At the group therapist's suggestion, she brought her child to a gestalt therapist who worked with children. She spoke as if her financial resources were limited and as if it were a fact that she would not need to be involved in her son's problems. The child therapist did not listen to the rumblings of disquiet he was hearing within himself. He agreed to treat her son and to not require her to become involved herself in the therapeutic relationship. He satisfied himself with the hope that the therapeutic work she would be doing in her group would be sufficiently useful to permit him to proceed with the child alone. This was a mistake. It almost always is. Even though in personal therapy, a parent does not necessarily work on problems which have direct and immediate bearing on his relationship with the child, or the timing of such work may not be appropriate to dealing with the child in his own situation. When a child is in individual therapy, it is most usually desirable that the parent be seen *specifically* in reference to his relationship with the child. This of course does usually lead to working out unfinished problems which also affect the parent generally, but the child-parent relationship is not lost sight of.

The symptoms this mother had described were dramatic. Although in good health, her son experienced phases of weakness, of almost fainting, and panic-like fears of dying. He acknowledged those symptoms and wanted help about them. He had recently left the home of his father, who lived in a different state, and had come to live with his mother. His brother had remained with their father. The therapist saw the child individually four times or so. They were on good terms with each other, but the therapist found himself uncomfortable with the child's frequently going into activities, in their meetings, which were obvious withdrawals from the conflictful and painful areas he and his mother had presented. The therapist then made a belated attempt to involve the mother in the treatment process. He asked the mother and child to work jointly with him. The mother was willing; the child reluctantly agreed but would not work with his reluctance. In the joint sessions this mother displayed acute, intense, sometimes direct, and somtimes indirect, but almost unrelenting hostility to her son concerning his lack of communication with her. The therapist could guess that the pain she felt at her son's distress, and at what she conceived to be her own part in eliciting it, was itself acute and turned into acute anger in reaction to her son's self-protective silence. The son, in return, suffered enough himself that, spontaneously, he physically left each of the three joint sessons, and he asked after the very first joint session to stop therapy—somewhat, it appeared, in retaliation to his mother's attacks, though probably more as an avoidance of pain. The problem areas which the parent and child had originally described were dramatic in themselves; but especially dramatic, and more to the foreground, were the painfully conflicting aspects of the child-parent relationship—and the underlying attitudes and emotions. Whenever a parent is exceedingly hostile to the child, not only must the parent be involved in the treatment program from the beginning, but also he must be seen separately from the child. As he works through his own pain and anger in reference to his child and in reference to any relevant unfinished situations from the past, he can give increasing leeway to the child to become himself and to profit from the therapeutic contacts. Joint sessions can later on be feasible.

By working with the parents, the therapist acknowledges the child's dependency. By extension, the child is also realistically dependent on the therapist. The child's dependency becomes part of the relationship and needs to be included in the therapeutic context.

When parents bring the child to the therapist they are, by the fact of bringing him there, trying to share and/or delegate their powers to the therapist. This is especially true when the parents are aware that their relationship with the child plays a part in how he functions. The therapist, by accepting the case is accepting some of these powers, though not necessarily all. While the parents are likely to be ambivalent about this delegation of power, what in effect they may be saying to the child is: "What your therapist says and does is ok by us. We know he may say or do things that are different from or contrary to the ways we have been acting, but we trust him to do what's right. We want him to undo our influence when it has been detrimental to you and to supplement it where we have been lacking." Hence the therapist, in the child's view, is invested with some power to counter the destructive taboos and shoulds which the child has incorporated through his daily experience in his familial environment. The therapist, however, must remember his limitations when he works with the child: that his exercise of his power depends upon the parents' willingness, that he is not the parent, and that the child lives with and is dependent upon the parents. Also, how the therapist relates with the child and the parents significantly affects whether the parents continue their therapeutic effort. The gestalt therapeutic work with the parents and with the child are both aimed at creating opportunities for the child to increase his self-support, his self-viability, and his self-realization.

The reality of the dependence of children on adults also encompasses the area of values. I believe that most child therapists consider it a fact that children are very susceptible to evaluating themselves relative to the adults they depend on. If parents prevalently experience their child as being of little worth, the child tends to acquire this value of himself. If parents experience their child as worthwhile, or as bringing forth their esteem only when his behavior conforms to their values, the child's own sense of worth will be thus influenced. If parents esteem their child greatly but experience themselves as inferior, their child, through his identification with his parents, and in spite of their great esteem for him, will tend to develop underlying feelings of inferiority, of worthlessness as compared with people not in his family. Naturally, many other factors are involved in a child's development, but the dependency factor is one of the important ones. Hence, the gestalt therapist who is aware of how his reality impinges on that of the child will be more willing to be supportive by expressing his reality, so that his own esteem and respect for the child will experientially spark or validate the child's own self-esteem. Dorothy Baruch's description of her work (1966, p. 38) with a little boy contains a vividly written incident where her positive view of a child's maleness obviously contributes to the child's correctively experiencing himself as a male. With adults, however, gestalt therapists would tend to be more insistent that the client himself, rather than the therapist, be the greater source of self-realization.

Perhaps obviously, even this is a relative matter. The gestalt therapist working with adults, by his own evident respect for the client's potential when he refuses to be "helpful," does contribute to supporting self-realization in the client. Furthermore, when working in groups, the gestalt therapist frequently occasions the group members to feed back to the client their own perceptions of him, thereby providing a certain measure of externally derived experiences which frequently contribute to the client's positive evolvement. With children, however, the therapist must make it evident to the child that it is now safe to move in the direction of self-realization, and to make evident the therapist's positive feelings when the child does so. Generally, the child more than the adult (except perhaps the prevalently psychotic adult) needs this external source of validation to permit himself to incorporate an appreciation of himself. He can then become progressively more and more self-supporting.

On the other hand, if the child's environment is still unsafe in terms of the child's self-realization, the Gestalt therapist must of course respect this reality. While feeling and expressing some sympathy for the child's plight is supporting and validating to the child, dwelling on the plight incites or reinforces in the child the feeling and belief of helplessness. However, the extent and nature of the dangers involved are often very vague to the child. They may translate themselves into a general sense of foreboding which is quite pervasive. Offering the child opportunities to define for himself and experience in fantasy the actual dimensions of such dangers permits him to come in greater contact with himself and with the actual dangers involved. This process affords him the opportunity to increase his self-support in ways compatible with his survival in a given environment.

Another fact which makes it desirable that the parent be involved therapeutically specifically in reference to the child, is the need the parent usually experiences to be kept informed in a tangible way as to whether or not the therapeutic process is going well. This must be done, without betraying the child's confidences, in order for the parent to understand and trust the therapist's efforts. This often involves also meaningfully educating the parent as to how the child's contacts with the therapist are useful.

Another reason for making provisions for child-centered therapist-parent conferences is for the therapist to keep himself informed as to what is happening in the child's life that is relevant to the child's personal experience and growth.

Whether, in relation to these child-centered sessions, parents see the child's therapist or another therapist who closely collaborates with the child's therapist, depends upon both clinical and practical considerations.

Clinical considerations would involve such concerns as the following. If a child client or his parent tends to be markedly paranoid, would two therapists rather than one, or one rather than two, be best? If a parent is much prejudiced against his working with a male or female therapist, would it be best to initially cater to this prejudice or try to work it through? Or does the therapist personally happen to have a difficult time working with the parent? Practical considerations involve such questions as availability of therapist, availability of parents, financial considerations, distance child and parents must travel, etc.

SOME EXAMPLES OF GESTALT-ORIENTED INTERACTION, AND SOME COMMENTS

Pain. In *Gestalt Therapy Verbatim*, Perls states (1969, pp. 52-53) that the " . . . enemy of development is this pain phobia—the unwillingness to do a tiny bit of suffering . . . . in therapy the person might simply become phobic and run away . . . ." The example I have just related about the eleven-year-old boy illustrates the need to work therapeutically with the child's parents. However, it also illustrates the need to heed Perls's observation concerning pain phobia.

If pain phobia is in the foreground, it is pain phobia that the therapist must be willing to deal with and take into account. Generally, children have a lower tolerance for pain than adults do, or are less well defended against it. When doing family therapy, I often make this point clear at the offset, both with the parents and the children. This facilitates my doing something to take account of the child's lesser tolerance for pain: giving him a chance to withdraw physically or emotionally from the situation. This process then acknowledges and validates him and his pain with little risk of parental retaliation. However and also to the point, I give the child opportunities to learn to support himself, so that he himself will openly initiate his giving himself a break, a time to withdraw, a time to rest. This is not to say that family sessions are usually excessively painful—but they sometimes are.

Some of the theories which are part of Gestalt Therapy do obviously permeate our daily lives when they become part of the ways we perceive ourselves and our world. I would like to mention in passing two small incidents involving individual parental attitudes.

Playing. One afternoon a child and his father were playing kickball in the alley behind their house. They were feeling fine, both in regard to themselves and to each other. They were kicking the ball to each other. The child was getting a little upset as the ball he kicked often went to the left and "out" when he wanted it to go straight.

What did the father do? Scold his child for not paying attention? Tell him to straighten out his foot? Tell him it didn't matter? Tell him that he probably wanted to lose? Tell him that he probably didn't want to play? Acknowledge that the child was a bit upset? Encourage him to try harder? Ignore the situation? Tell him he was just trying to get attention? Or that perhaps he was simply tired? Say he'd probably do better next time? Or say that perhaps he would feel uncomfortable winning? Did he suggest they stop playing? Or examine how the child holds his foot and make corrective suggestions as to how the child ought to modify his stance? Some of these responses would probably be useful to the child, especially if the father continued to feel good toward him.

In this instance the father, perceiving apparently correctly that the child might want help or be open to it, suggested that the child go along with his tendency and kick the ball to the left and "out" *on purpose* a few times. The child did so, and he then kicked the ball straight consistently for awhile. He repeated the "on purpose" experiment one more time and had no more difficulty that afternoon. Whatever the basic nature of his difficulty—perceptual-motor, or emotional, or both—either his willingness to *stay with it* and *go along with it* or his father's willingness for him to go along with it, or a combination of both, permitted the boy to proceed from the confusion, frustration, and impasse of wanting to kick the ball straight and yet making it go crooked.

Fear. On a sunny day an eleven-year-old girl was playing in a swimming pool. Her mother was sitting by the pool. Both were on good terms with each other, and each was pleasantly passing the time of day. The child swam to her mother and said something like, "You know, Mom, at the end of the pool where the water gets drained out through that hole with the grill on it? Well, it makes a funny sucking noise and I get scared when I come close to it." Of course various mothers respond differently, and differently on different days and moments depending on their mood, on what they are doing, on their relationship with their daughter at that time, or whatever.

On this specific occasion, this mother responded in a way which reflected gestalt principles and techniques. She suggested that her daughter go back toward that drain hole, let herself be scared, and exaggerate her feeling of fear. The child did so and had a fun time exaggerating her fear. And she stopped being scared.

Some illustrations follow of therapy with children where a gestalt approach is involved in the interaction.

Nightmare. A young girl awakened almost nightly with nightmares of being chased or kidnapped. Rather than being asked to associate to the various aspects of her dream, and rather than interpreting it, this child was asked to act out the various elements of her nightmare. She did so with gusto, with the therapist eventually involving himself in the dream by portraying the child as the child clued him to portray her, while the child became the kidnapper. In this instance it became obvious to the child that the kidnapper had no intent of hurting her, but wanted her for himself. (The child, among other conflicts, was in the midst of a power struggle as to whom—her divorced mother or father—would prevail over her, and the child herself had ambivalent preferences.) This nightmare was reenacted during several sessions, at the child's instigation.

Cheating. A child consistently cheated when playing checkers with the therapist. The therapist was aware of his own feelings and of the child's behavior when he cheated. "I just saw you smiling when you did such and such," the therapist said. "What did you feel?" The child replied that he felt good. As this interaction recurred, it became more evident that the child felt pleasure not so much at winning as at hoodwinking the therapist. The therapist went along with this and, with the child's knowledge, pretended to be hoodwinked a good many times, with the child responding with great glee. The child began to accept his own want and enjoyed it freely. This led to further interaction around the child's experiences of hoodwinking and being hoodwinked.

Cheating. Another child consistently cheated when playing checkers or similar games with the therapist. This child briefly acknowledged his extreme pleasure at winning and extreme disturbance at losing. The therapist, with the child's knowledge, then helped the child cheat and win. The child began to become more and more flowing with his feelings and less "driven" as he played.

Sometimes the child will speak of his pain at always seeming to be the loser in his interpersonal transactions, and sometimes he will not verbalize such experiences. Either way, in sessions such as these he experiences openly and expresses openly his wants and feelings in respect to winning and losing, and this is so regardless of whether or not he fully articulates them in words. Such expressions and experiences of openly realizing his wants permit him to move on instead of remaining stuck and continuing to repeat the same pattern.

Controlling. A child was "controlling" his therapist. He said, "Let's do this, that, now you do this, that, no do it this way, no don't do that, do this, now watch me," etc., etc. The child controlled automatically. The therapist felt subdued, smothered. The therapist then declined to do as the boy told him to, and expressed how he felt at that moment. Several times, however—and perhaps many other times—he did offer the child the opportunity to deliberately tell him what to do for awhile. The child progressively became aware of what he was doing and his feeling as he controlled. While with the therapist, the child's attempts at controlling were no longer a "no-no" eliciting antagonism. He was able to freely live and experience his wanting to control. Progressively, his wanting to control lost its quality of being an unintegrated part of himself that constantly came to life without any relationship to the other realities of the situation.

Feeling unloving as a parent. Some parents read how-to books on parenting and profit a little or much from reading them, and lastingly so. Some profit for a few days or hours or weeks, or for no time at all. The same two statements are true in reference to advice given face to face by professionals: psychologists, pediatricians, counselors, psychiatrists.

When parents, try as they may, are unable to acquire attitudes they believe would be good for them to hold toward their children, it is likely that such attitudes, regardless of how desirable they might be, are organismically incompatible with them.

A mother felt unloving toward her nine-year-old daughter, though loving toward her other children. Each morning she let this child provoke her into a fight, which was often the only personal contact they had all day long. In the mother's session one day, the therapist requested she address the child (actually a pillow sitting on a chair) to tell the child how she disliked her, did not want to touch her, and other aversive feelings. She then became silent, stating she was blank. She remained so for a while, then saw herself as a child, wanting her father's love, trying to get it by showing him good grades and behaving properly—then giving up any attempt at receiving affection from him. She identified herself with her own child, the one she was willing to touch only under the command of her own "should." It was as if she had transposed to her child her own numbness to her wants for affection from her parent.

The woman then accepted the therapist's homework: to view her child before she was ready to wake her up in the morning, and to silently assert to herself she was going to deny loving that child just as she had denied to herself wanting to be loved. After a few mornings of this she felt like hugging the child as she woke her up in the morning. Apparently this warm contact took the place of the fighting contacts they had had daily. This of course is an oversimplified statement of an actual happening. The mother had much more work to do toward resolving her "unfinished business" with her father.

Withdrawal in fantasy. During family sessions a seven-year-old girl's responses to her parents were characterized by indirectness. So much so that at times there seemed to be, on the surface at least, no connection between the child's response and the parent's statement. At best, her responses were peripheral, tangential. She fairly frequently seemed to withdraw into her own world. Her mother would get upset and irritated, her father upset and ascerbic. The situation duplicated what was going on at home.

On one occasion when the child was seemingly withdrawn, the therapist inquired about the child's immediate experience. She related then a fantasy of planets whirling in space, passing each other, or intersecting each other, but always at a great distance from each other, never close, so that they would not crash into each other and be destroyed. This expression of her fantasy brought the child and parents closer together. The parents felt moved. They became knowing of the child, and the child more knowing of herself. The child then directly verbalized her fears and concerns about confronting her father directly.

THERAPEUTIC MODALITIES AND TECHNIQUES—THEIR USE IN GESTALT THERAPY WITH CHILDREN

Before the clinician recommends or undertakes psychotherapy relative to a child, he usually has already evaluated the overall situation. Frequently this evaluation may simply involve a couple of sessions with the child, his parents, and his siblings, individually or together. On occasion the evaluation will additionally involve consultation with the school staff (if the child has special social or academic problems), or consultation with the child's physician (if, say, the child has encopresis, persistent headaches, or other physical symptoms), or an evaluation of the child's academic skills by a learning disability specialist or psychometric and/or projective testing for a variety of circumstances.

It may turn out that psychotherapy is the only recommended process, or it may be part of a number of remediative processes (tutoring, physical therapy, etc.)

Having recommended therapy, the clinician must also formulate a tentative plan as to which of the available modalities would be best to begin with—group therapy, individual, family, separate sessions for the parents, group work or individual for the parents—and what combination of these would probably be best in the initial phases; which of course implies that one would be open to changes as the situation evolved.

As is evident from the above, the general context within which psychotherapy takes place is usually more complex with children than with adults. This then is another of the differences in working with children, as compared with working with adults.

However, the key point is that whatever therapeutic modalities are used, what makes them "gestalt" is *how* the therapist uses them, *how* he perceives, *how* he reacts. The modality itself is irrelevant. The same can be said about techniques—work with dreams or fantasies can be gestalt or can be something else. The interaction between the patient and therapist can reflect gestalt therapy ways of perceiving or may reflect other points of view. Some techniques, however, are typical of gestalt therapy, such as the face-to-face method developed by James Simkin, or the topdog/underdog interaction developed by Perls.

Different techniques are used with children depending on their ages, on how verbal they are, on which modes of interaction they have an affinity for, on the therapist's own predilections and skills, on the circumstances of the moment. Without losing sight of the fact that it is basically how the therapist is or is not which characterizes the "gestaltness" of the therapeutic process, I shall comment briefly on some of the main therapeutic vehicles and techniques for doing therapy with children.

Therapeutic questions. During ongoing activities and interaction, such focal questions as, "What are you feeling now,"

"Where in your body are you feeling this?" can, I find, be easily used fruitfully.

Going-along-with. Purposeful repetition, symbolic enactment, or exaggeration of self- or other-alienating types of behavior are easily used techniques. Instances of such use would be cheating on purpose, destroying a drawn replica of the therapist's office instead of actually kicking its walls, controlling the therapist by mutual consent, or kicking a cardboard box instead of another boy in the group.

Awareness continuum. Whereas I like at times using this technique with adults I hardly ever find myself comfortable using it with children. In fact, I quickly gave up considering using it. This may be my own particularity, but I believe I am accurate in sensing that for various reasons this technique is basically unsuited for use with most children. Nor have I found other Gestalt therapists mentioning using this technique in their work with children (Cohn, 1970; Kempler, 1973; Lederman, 1970; Rhyne, 1973).

I am not referring, of course, to bringing the child's attention to what he is experiencing. I am referring to the *constant, continued* attempt to have the patient register and express what he is experiencing.

This technique has been almost a trademark of the gestalt therapist. I regretted finding it impractical with children. And I still do at times feel such regret. Perls's remarks (1973, p. 85) helped console me:

> There is . . . one obvious limitation to the awareness technique used alone. It would probably take years to achieve its results, as do most of the orthodox therapies . . . But, having recognized the relationship between fantasy and actuality, we can make full use in therapy of fantasizing and all its increasing states of intensity towards actuality—a verbalized fantasy, or one which is written down, or one which is acted out as psychodrama.

Dreams. Children usually respond very well to the gestalt methods of working with this type of fantasy.

Play fantasy without props. Often, children spontaneously produce fantasies which are expressive of their wants and fears. The therapist goes along with them, permits them to unfold. When the child involves the therapist in the fantasy so that each is enacting different roles and functions, it is quite feasible for the therapist to request a reversal of roles.

Dolls, puppets, etc. Fantasies mediated with props, such as dolls and trucks and animals, also lend themselves well to the child's expressing, experiencing, and owning his attitudes and emotions.

Story telling. Either triggered from pictures or made purely out of one's imagination, such fantasies are often easily elicited. As in everything else, the gestalt therapist is attuned to how the child tells the stories (affective and motor expression) as well as to what he is saying.

Art work. This lends itself well to the Gestalt orientation (Rhyne, 1973).

Interpersonal encounters. Children respond very well to this therapeutic mode. The interpersonal encounter which obviously lends itself so well to the I-and-thou, here-and-now principles of gestalt therapy is eminently applicable in family therapy. However, this technique can be destructive when the therapist is not attuned to the sometimes exceedingly high hostility harbored by family members toward each other, or when he is unable to limit its expression.

As an aside, I want to add in regard to family therapy that I found it useful to have available any of the techniques available to a Gestalt therapist, including dream work, going-along-with, etc.

The interpersonal encounter technique is naturally also employed in group therapy with children. And of course interpersonal encounters would naturally take place with the gestalt therapist whether it be in individual, group, or family therapy.

Intrapersonal encounters. Such direct encounters as topdog/underdog, or the scared part of me vs. the angry part of me, can sometimes be used with some children, but I find them a bit too difficult for most. Enactment of fantasies, through various media, can be used more easily to the same end.

Movement. With children clients, motoric expression is usually spontaneous and occurs during various activities—fantasy with props or without, even during story telling, or during going-along-with repetitions and exaggerations. So it is therefore usually easy for the gestalt child therapist to encourage motoric expression. Some children are motorically limp or rigidly tense, and with them, movement need be suggested and requires more work to elicit.

There is a short film (*Looking for Me*, 1970) in which mirroring of a client's movement and, much later on in therapy, movement originated by the therapist, were employed as the major therapeutic mode with very young, autistic children. I found the interaction and evolvement of the interaction marvelous to watch. Nothing in the narrative of the film led me to believe that the technique was overtly associated with Gestalt Therapy. However, it seemed to me that this was Gestalt Therapy *par excellence:* sheer poetry in the I-you and here-and-now dimensions.

As Naranjo states (1972, p. 3),

> The techniques of gestalt therapy are many and cover a wide spectrum of behaviors—verbal and non-verbal, structured and unstructured, introspective and interpersonal, inner and outer-directed, symbolic and non-symbolic. Some of these techniques are not unique to gestalt therapy and perhaps every one of them may be regarded as a variation (intentional or not) upon a technique to be found in an alternative form of psychotherapy or in some system of spiritual guidance . . . In his lifetime Perls increased his repertoire with anything that served his aim of making his patients more aware and responsible. He adapted, borrowed, combined and never ceased to invent techniques, not deliberately, but with the spontaneous assimilation-creation of life itself.

In conclusion, I want to say that I am enthusiastic about Gestalt Therapy as it relates to children.

The three major factors that I mentioned as differentiating Gestalt Therapy work with adults from work with children are part of reality and part of the process of life. Gestalt Therapy, by its very emphasis on reality, on the here-and-now, on the you-and-I, and on the dynamic relationship of foreground to background, is eminently suited theoretically to doing effective work with children in the context of their lives with their parents.

Similarly, in reference to the Gestalt Therapy imprint on therapeutic techniques, the very affinity which Gestalt Therapy has for these dimensions, as well as its focus on full organismic experience, goes well with the affinity which children have for rehearsing, expressing, and experiencing through fantasy and movement. Gestalt Therapy is by its very nature well suited to contribute to the modification, evolvement, and development of therapeutic techniques and attitudes in the field of psychotherapy with children.

REFERENCES

Baruch, D. Little mockingbird. In Clark Moustakas (Ed.) *Existential Child Therapy.* New York: Basic Books, Inc., 1966. pp. 30-44.

Cohn, C. A child with stomachache: Fusion of psychoanalytic concepts and Gestalt techniques, in Fagan, J. and Shepherd, I. L., Eds. *Gestalt Therapy Now.* Palo Alto, Calif.: Science and Behavior Books, 1970.

Fagan, J. The third degree impasse and schizophrenia. *Voices,* 1974, 10, No. 2, pp. 4-6.

Kempler, W. *Principles of Gestalt Family Therapy.* Oslo, Norway: Nordahls Trykkeri, 1973.

Lederman, J. Anger and the rocking chair, in Fagan, J. and Shepherd, L. S., Eds., *Gestalt Therapy Now.* Palo Alto, Calif.: Science and Behavior Books, 1970.

Looking For Me. Film. Written and narrated by Janet Adler. Producers: Virginia Bartlett and Norris Brock for the Shady Lane School of Pittsburgh, Pennsylvania, 1970. Music: Carol Saunders. Black and white. 29 minutes. Distributors: Multi Media Resource Center, Inc., 540 Powell Street, San Francisco, Calif., 94108

Naranjo, C. *The Techniques of Gestalt Therapy.* Berkeley, Calif.: The SAT Press, 1972.

Perls, F. S. *Gestalt Therapy Verbatim.* Morb, Ut.: Real People Press, 1969.

Perls, F. S. *The Gestalt Approach and Eye Witness to Therapy.* USA: Science and Behavior Books, Inc., 1973.

Rhyne, J. *The Gestalt Art Experience.* Belmont, Calif.: Wadsworth Publishing Company, Inc., 1973.

GRASS-ROOTS GESTALT

John Elliot, B.S. and Vickie Ficht, B.S.

In our experience, gestalt therapy can be used effectively with a grass-roots client population. We define grass-roots by certain basic characteristics of the client, such as low income, little or no education, lack of communication and problem-solving skills, lack of external supports (employment, family, etc.), little or no concept of affective growth, and motivations for change controlled by external sources. Such people are often unaware of the advantages in knowing themselves and their feelings.

Many of these clients are from oppressed minority groups or are involved in crime and/or drug and alcohol abuse. In many instances they have been required to seek counseling by the criminal justice system, the welfare system, or schools. Therefore we see many resistant clients who see no value in therapy. In fact most clients have already had negative experiences in therapy previous to our contact.

In dealing with the grass-roots client we work from a larger gestalt than the gestalt session itself. This is an approach which can enhance the use of therapeutic techniques, although we always keep in mind that the relationship between counselor and client takes priority over the best techniques. Some of the constructs relevant to this approach are trust, modeling, readiness, pressure, reinforcement, directiveness, limits, environment, and contact.

Because gestalt is a very creative and flexible mode of therapy, styles of gestalt therapists tend to vary. Some use group pressure to force down defenses. Others use frustration as a primary tool for breaking through an impasse. Manipulations may also be used as part of the therapeutic process. We find these orientations usually ineffective with the population we work with. So many other people in their lives have used these methods to motivate the client, that they resist because of their bad experiences. For us, the client's sense of control is very important. We want him to learn to be sure of himself and to be aware that he can control himself in a therapy situation. Group supportiveness is encouraged, as is the personal involvement of the therapist in revealing his own feelings (although too many words of support or too much initial self-expression may be seen as phony or mushy). Flexibility in the use of techniques such as psychodrama, imagery, body therapy, and behavior modification has proven very successful. We believe this is because in these modes there is a lack of heavy judgment about right or wrong.

One of the major difficulties we have encountered among clients is the lack of personal motivation to change. They see no advantages in changing. Many have never had a healthy role model, so do not know what positive personality traits are. Our approach can be very attractive to these clients, because of lack of pressure to be verbal or to meet the therapist's expectations. Clients move at their own pace and generally enjoy the variety of interactions, facilitated by the use of different techniques.

Because of the severity of the client's problems, there is a tendency for the therapist to focus too much energy on the client without taking care of himself. It just seems natural to become involved when someone comes in who has been in prison for eighteen out of thirty years, is hungry, angry, using heroin daily, and his wife is prostituting. The heavy focus on the client appears to be one factor leading to what is commonly know as being "burned out." The therapist becomes drained, frustrated, and angry, often wishing to give up. He needs to constantly focus on himself, to be aware of how his own feelings are affecting the interaction with the client. Many clients work on problems as yet unresolved within the therapist. For instance, a therapist who is an exaddict may not be clear and perceptive in working with drug clients because of his own unfinished business with the drug scene. Consequently, the client may become fixed at a particular phase of his development, or the therapist may project his past experience to the client. An awareness of this process is extremely important, so that the therapist can adjust the type of interaction with the client. Adjustments may include starting a new pattern of self-revealing responses; switching to nonverbal, body, or imagery techniques; consulting another therapist on a theoretical or experiential level; or even transferring the client.

READINESS

By readiness, we mean the ability of both client and therapist to deal with a specific level of client problem. Each client, for whatever reasons, may be either more or less prepared to deal with intense problems in a short period of time. If the therapist pursues a problem focus too quickly, the client may not be able to fully integrate his work. If the therapist does not pursue work quickly enough, the client's willingness to work on deeper levels of his problem may deteriorate. Further work in this particular area may become even more blocked.

One way of determining client readiness is to ask the client directly whether he wants to go deeper. This has the added attraction of enhancing the client's feelings of control and responsibility. For example:

T. I see that we have really dealt with a lot of issues concerning your divorce, and I would like to know if you want to go a little deeper.

C. Yes, I am sick and tired of being like this. What do I do now? (or) No, I have done a lot for today.

Another aspect of readiness is related to individual and group work. It is a rare occurrence for us to place individuals directly into a group setting. The level of trust is usually extremely low at first contact, and exposure to intense group work can frighten clients away. We have a general policy of seeing individuals in private sessions before placing them into groups, to develop trust and expose them to new concepts and techniques.

REINFORCEMENT

Many of our clients are involved in extreme attention-getting behavior when we first see them. This behavior may polarize into either detailed accounts of violence or complete withdrawal. Many studies have shown that conditioning takes place constantly in our everyday lives. Eye contact, a touch, or a nod of the head all serve as a powerful reinforcement in shaping behavior. Rather than ignoring these tools because they are "ungestalt," we use them. We try to be constantly aware of what the client actually wants, and reinforce those qualitites or behaviors the client is trying to achieve for himself. When the counselor reinforces his own values rather than the client's values, change in the client's attitude and behavior last only as long as he is in contact with the reinforcer. This may explain why some programs or therapists seem to be very successful, but after clients leave, they go back to old patterns.

In order to continue taking care of ourselves, we consciously reinforce only the behavior we are comfortable with. By no means does this imply that we always agree with the client. However, we do trust the client's capability for self-regulation in most cases.

It is important that at least one significant other, especially the therapist, accept the client for who he is. The therapist may be the only person that the client has encountered during his life who will reinforce him for being himself. It is very common to hear clients talk about themselves as always having been the "black sheep" and say that they have never pleased anyone. The unfinished business from traumatic childhood experiences is common as a focus. Being the darkest-skinned child in a Mexican family may be a cause of problems and a label which lasts until he deals with it in group. Being ugly, dumb, or poor leads to feelings of rejection, causing a person to fall into a role such as "one who is rejected."

TRUST

Trust seems to be the foremost lack among grass-roots clients—both trust of others and trust of themselves. A strong effort must be made by the therapist to allow the client to learn to trust both him and the group. An immediate responsiveness on the part of the therapist to gain his client's confidence may produce a negative impact on the relationship, and the client may withdraw and reject real contact.

We define trust as a feeling of safety and confidence. The consistency of the therapist may be one of the most important factors in developing trust-keeping confidences; preventing other group members from dumping (blaming), and maintaining time limits for sessions are part of this consistency. Another important factor is the extent to which the therapist trusts the client. If the therapist feels threatened, this feeling will be communicated to the client. In such a situation, it seems best to mention it, and still let the client know that you are in control of yourself. There are also different degrees of trust that a client may experience in relation to the therapist. From the client's perspective the therapist may indeed not be worth trusting.

Values vary among socioeconomic, cultural, and age levels. What the therapist considers trustworthy, i.e., honesty, openness, contact, and consistency, may be unimportant to the client. Perhaps hiding him out from the police, giving him money, or lying to a probation officer may be the only trusting behavior.

It is a very sad fact that the therapist may indeed be the only person to give the client genuine concern and support. This matter needs to be treated very delicately. Most of our clients lack the ability to differentiate feelings for the opposite sex. Feelings toward the therapist often become sexual. Therefore the therapist needs to be aware of this process and make his feelings and intentions explicit. Intentions and feelings may be very different. A therapist may feel sexual toward the client and have no intention of making sexual contact. The client may resist the fact that the therapist really cares for him or her if the therapist does not want intimate contact.

This may be a period when the client withdraws and takes time to adjust. This may take five seconds or five weeks. It may also be an unconscious attempt to break contact in the therapeutic setting, since spending time as lovers rather than client/therapist might indeed allow the client to avoid confronting his problems.

One attractive female therapist experienced almost a regular phase in therapy where male clients would approach her sexually and then withdraw when her intentions of wanting only a therapeutic relationship became explicit. A conversation between therapist and client might go something like this:

C. There's something I've been wanting to tell you for a long time. I am attracted to you and I want to go to bed with you.

T. I feel good that you like me a lot. I feel good with you and I don't want to go to bed with you, even though I feel close, warm, and affectionate sometimes.

C. I'm just another client to you. You get paid to see me and now I know you don't care.

T. I do care, and I don't want to have a sexual relationship with you.

This client left therapy without a call and returned after three weeks. He resumed therapy and was even more involved than before, because his previously unexpressed feelings and concern over rejection had now become his focus.

ENVIRONMENT

It is important to understand the environment that our clients come from. It may be important from time to time for a therapist who is financially secure and well-educated to role-play his clients in order to keep in touch with feelings of theirs that may be very different from his own. Home and school visits can help the therapist understand the client better. Developing body awareness, living in the here and now, taking responsibility, being direct, and expressing feelings may be inappropriate and dangerous in the environment these clients live in. We stress to them that behavior appropriate in therapy may not be appropriate outside. For instance, smiling and expressing warmth in the group is accepted. But on the street it may be seen in both men and women as weakness and therefore may attract emotional or physical abuse.

The client's family and peers may have a strong investment in his not changing. A young boy or girl may be used as the scapegoat for harshness and resentment by a parent who has problems at work. If the child begins to change and become more normal, the parents won't have anyone to blame and release their aggression on. Therefore we discuss and work on the reality that healthy expression of feelings in certain situations may only hurt them when interacting in their present environment.

The client may also be in a dependent situation and lack the financial or social mobility to fulfill needs discovered through therapy. A client who realizes he needs to move out of the community may not have any money, legal status, or method of obtaining funds to move. The therapist must therefore proceed at a very cautious pace. The client needs time to adjust his environment or build the necessary strength to fulfill these needs. Additional sessions may be necessary so that specific discussion concerning these adjustments may take place.

If the therapist proceeds too quickly in opening the client to deep, unwanted feelings, without environmental support, the client may be worse off than before starting therapy. We see the client's defenses as being very delicate protections that they have used for many years to protect themselves from unbearable pain. Blasting away these defenses would leave the client vulnerable and weakened until he or she finds positive replacement.

One example of this kind of vulnerability is an exaddict who entered therapy to hopefully prevent his returning to heroin. Within two sessions he became deeply aware of his aloneness and sadness. He was unprepared to deal with these feelings, as he had not yet developed social skills to fulfill his previously unrecognized needs. Having no skill in making friends or expressing needs to others, he remained very lonely. Consequently he returned to heroin to escape the feeling. A more ideal process would have been to explore patterns of dealing with loneliness before allowing him to experience those deep emotional levels.

The client's involvement in new interests or activities may be one means of developing an external support system. As the client grows, he will also have a greater need to express himself creatively. Community centers, social groups, art museums, and spiritual or religious gatherings can provide both support and alternate modes of expression.

Our clients are constantly fighting labels such as "crazy," "criminal," and "dope fiend." The therapist may want to educate or request help from others in the client's environment, especially families. For example, a father who does not respect his son's sensitivity, such as when the boy cries, may simply be asked not to verbalize judgment of his son's behavior in the son's presence. This way the negative reinforcement is kept at a minimum. Educating families, teacher, probation officers, and police to the causes and treatment of antisocial behavior is often necessary in order to obtain cooperation. A probation officer may automatically see a drug user as "born bad" and think that no one ever really changes. Informing him of other cases in which therapy has been successful often is all he needs to begin referring clients to therapy instead of jail.

LIMITS

Something very apparent to us is that significant others in the client's life do not set and maintain limits of acceptable behavior. In the family environment the first sign of a juvenile's desire for more consistent limits occurs as acting-out behavior, such as shoplifting, truancy or paint sniffing. If the child knows that the parent is unwilling to set limits to control his acting-out, he also has no assurance that his parents will place limits to insure his safety and security. The therapist must also set limits for these reasons.

Here are some quotes from youth from the Mid Cities Drug Counseling in Fort Worth, Texas: *Don't spoil me* (I know quite well that I ought not to have all that I ask for. I'm testing you.) *Don't be afraid to be firm with me* (I prefer it; it makes me feel more secure.) *Don't let me feel smaller than I am* (It only makes me behave stupidly "big.") *Don't correct me in front of people if you can help it* (I'll take much more notice if you talk quietly with me in private.) *Don't make me feel my mistakes are sins* (It upsets my sense of values.) *Don't protect me from consequences* (I need to learn the painful way sometimes.) *Don't be upset when I say "I hate you"* (It isn't you I hate but your power to thwart me.) *Don't take too much notice of my small ailments* (Sometimes they get me the attention I need.) *Don't nag* (If you do, I shall have to protect myself by appearing deaf.) *Don't forget I cannot explain myself as well as I like* (This is why I'm not always very accurate.) *Don't make rash promises* (Remember that I feel badly let down when promises are broken.) *Don't tax my honesty too much* (I am easily frightened into telling lies.) *Don't be inconsistent* (That completely confuses me and makes me lose faith in you.) *Don't tell me my fears are silly* (They are terribly real and you can do much to reassure me if you try to understand.) *Don't put me off when I ask questions* (If you do, you will find that I stop asking and seek my information elsewhere.) *Don't ever suggest that you are perfect or infallible* (It gives me too great a shock when I discover that you are neither.) *Don't think it is beneath your dignity to apologize to me* (An honest apology makes me feel surprisingly warm toward you.) *Don't forget how quickly I am growing up* (It must be very difficult to keep pace with me, but please try.) *Don't forget I love experimenting* (I couldn't get on without it, so please put up with it.) *Don't forget I can't thrive without understanding love* (But I don't need to tell you, do I.)

James Baldwin states that if the child is not told where his limits are he will spend the rest of his life trying to discover them. This includes therapy also. The process of acting-out or testing may also take place in the therapy session. It would be detrimental to the client if the therapist were inconsistent in his limits. By keeping this in mind, the therapist can be aware of a client's testing as part of the process of developing trust.

Consistency in general is especially important to grass-roots clients. An unexpected new group member or change in group schedule may strongly affect them and their involvement. They may close up or become resentful and not be willing to work it through.

PRESSURE

In our opinion, pressure is usually not effective in facilitating self-growth. Pressure may be effective in changing an individual, but the very nature of the client's change then becomes other-directed rather than self-directed. When someone wants to change, we find it's better if the person can change himself and not rely or depend on other people to change him—that is, to pressure him. Some clients only come to learn how to use the tools of gestalt and techniques and never really get into heavy gestalt work in the group itself. They sometimes later return to group and share their experience of doing self-therapy.

Since pressure can originate from either external or internal sources, it is extremely difficult to determine the degree of pressure any individual is experiencing. Too much pressure may already be causing a loss of motivation and feelings of hopelessness.

Many of our clients fit this category. There are constant demands on them, just to survive in their environment. Of course their facades of tough, mean, and bad may cover this.

We do not mean to imply that at times the use of pressures is to be totally rejected. We are speaking of the general approach and attitude toward the client. In our experience, if a therapist brings even more external pressure upon a client, responses of guilt and resentment usually lead to termination by the client.

MODELING

The feeling experience may be very new and awkward for the client. It is helpful if the therapist can give the client examples of emotional responses. An initial step is to provide clients with a vocabulary of emotional or affective terms, which can be discussed in depth. The therapist may also reflect the client's responses in more specific terms. For example:

C. My shoulders are up high and it feels funny here with you.

T. I imagine that your shoulders feel tense, and perhaps you feel uncomfortable with me.

The therapist may wish to expose his own feelings as a model for the client. The process of self-revealing should take place slowly. Clients from this population may be accustomed to "dumping," or blaming. Intense displays of genuine emotion may be frightening. We've seen gang leaders or gang members display hostility as a general characteristic, but react with tremendous fear over some genuine expression of emotion such as sadness, anger, or love.

DIRECTIVENESS

Since the majority of our clients are motivated by other people, it is necessary for us to be more directive during the first one or two months of therapy. When you've always been told what to do and how to be, it takes some adjustment to become aware that you have choices. The concept of individual choice is often alien to this population. They know, perhaps, what they don't want, or what probation wants, or what the school wants. When confronted with their right to choose, our clients become confused, insecure, and usually too unbalanced to remain with any focus. Many humanistic approaches seem to fail because of their lack of flexibility in this matter. They are not as directive as the client may initially need. Part of our process is to simply respond to where the client is. For example:

T. I see a lot of tension in your fist as we discuss your father. I would like to try an experiment now: Imagine the pillow is your father, and hit the pillow.

C. Come on, I feel really dumb.

T. (In a firm voice) Yes, I know you feel dumb and I want you to continue anyway.

At this point, if the client does not respond we would not pursue this particular means of expression. We might offer less threatening forms such as tearing paper or drawing.

As the client becomes comfortable and balanced, the therapist can gradually withdraw his directiveness and encourage increasing responsibility from him, especially for the direction of the work in therapy and the relationship between therapist and client.

CONCLUSION

The use of gestalt therapy is relatively new in dealing with the grass-roots client population. Therefore much of our work is experimental, and we continuously learn from our successes and mistakes. It is extremely important for the therapist to be aware of himself and to be flexible in the use of techniques when interacting with clients.

The problem of this population cannot be resolved in purely psychological ways. Problems in the environment, education, vocational background, and material needs must also be dealt with. The work we do with our clients is very difficult. We do not intend for our approach to provide easy answers or solutions. However, the work we do is very rewarding because our clients really are very sensitive, deep down inside, and are often just waiting for someone in their life to accept them. Gestalt is an excellent approach for working these deep-down feelings out into the light to be dealt with.

As therapists we go through many changes ourselves when working with clients. We experience love, fear, anger, sadness, and frustration at the needless injustices that are a daily part of our clients' lives. In working with them we have learned to accept and remain involved in the basic humanity that unites us all.

A GESTALT THERAPY APPROACH WITH CHILDREN THROUGH THE USE OF ART AND CREATIVE EXPRESSION

Violet Oaklander, Ph.D.

I would like to describe in this paper a method I have used with children, individually and in group, which consists of a variety of creative expressive techniques placed within a gestalt therapy framework. The focus of this method is to help the child build awareness of self. I attempt to help him or her experience fully the "now" of his experience and existence, to find out what he does in life, how he does it, and the consequences of these behaviors.

The techniques are interesting and enjoyable, a very important aspect of therapeutic work with children. Through art and other creative expressions, the child begins to openly express his or her inner world, a place that is usually very hidden and secret. Through this process, the child can discover and reveal her innermost feelings, and begins to clarify many anxieties, fears, unfinished situations, avoidances, and the many parts of herself. Through self-discovery—as the child learns about her own feelings, behaviors and attitudes—she begins to experience herself as a unique, valuable human being, with some control and choice for meeting her needs, and, in essence, for determining her own destiny. Through a new appreciation and sense of her own special self, an appreciation which emphasizes her own uniqueness, she begins to emerge and make contact with her world and the people in her world as an integrated, aware, responsible, dynamic, energetic, trusting, independent, exploring, feeling person. She finds that she is better able to cope with her world and deal with the reality problems of her life as they come along.

I use a great variety of activities and media, but the focus and purpose are always the same. Children enjoy doing many different kinds of things, and the child or a situation may lend itself to one kind of technique rather than another. It is essential to bear in mind that as any particular procedure is used, the therapist stays with the process that evolves with the child. The technique is a catalyst and is never to be regarded as a means to an end in itself. With this in mind, it then becomes clear that depending on the child (or children) and the situation, each session is unpredictable, and that one idea leads to another, that new techniques for creative expression are constantly evolving, and the therapeutic process is a dynamic, creative, open-ended one.

The techniques I have used have included drawings, painting, clay, collage, fantasy, stories, music, writing, poetry, play equipment, the sand tray, the chalk board, pictures, photographs, sculpture, dramatic play, wood work, comics, folklore, puppets, flannel-board figures, dreams, body movement, sensory awareness activities, string painting, finger painting, shells and driftwood, mosaic, plasticine, pla-do, scribble and squiggle drawings, gestalt games, active imagination, masks and costumes and hats, projective tests, hostility-venting devices, water. Each technique can be used in an endless variety of ways and in combinations. Although this may seem like a long list, there are many other kinds of ways that children can express themselves, and the children themselves often know far better than I do what they want to do, what they need to do, and how to do it.

It would be impossible to use all of these ideas with every child I work with, but they are there, together with others, for me to draw upon, depending on the age of the child or group of children, the situation, and the need. Many of these modes have been used with fairly well-adjusted children—*all* children enjoy and reap great benefit from creative activity. I have applied some of these techniques in therapeutic work with children who have had numerous problems including sibling conflicts, parental conflicts, withdrawal, isolation, social and interpersonal difficulties, extreme aggressiveness, hyperactivity, hypochondriasis, unexpressed (and in some cases, smoldering) anger, physical manifestation of anxiety (as tics), school difficulties, a variety of phobias and fears, inadequacies in communicating thoughts or ideas or particularly feelings, a pervasive low self-concept, frustration, and a general inability to cope with the pressures and demands of their environments. Through the use of these projective methods, children have been enabled to express openly and clarify their anxieties, fears, avoidances, frustrations, attitudes, patterns, manipulations, impulses, resistances, phobias, resentments, guilt feelings, wishes, wants, needs, and what I consider to be the core of their beings—feelings.

Often a child's outward behavior is misinterpreted as an expression of his or her real feelings. These real feelings are usually buried under a great mire of defensive behavior—behavior that may be unacceptable to the peers and adults in his or her life, but which is usually the child's way of fighting for his existence and very survival. This behavior —whether it be acting out, an "I don't care" stance, a non-communicative withdrawal into self, or some kind of physical symptom as bed wetting—is the child's way of using his vital energy toward a fight for life.

As the child unfolds, many things begin to happen. I as the therapist know that I need to assist the child in discovering new tools for dealing with life to replace the old, unrewarding behaviors that have usually served to bring him into therapy. Working with parents—and with teachers, since children spend half their lives in school—is certainly an important aspect of the therapeutic work. The child, himself, begins to gain strength and self-support for dealing with the many frustrations that accompany growing up in today's world. Some children, especially very young ones, do not necessarily need to verbalize their discoveries, experiences, intellectual insights, awarenesses of the what and how of their behaviors or feelings. Often it seems that by bringing out into the open, through some kind of expressions such as art, those blocked feelings which have interfered with the child's emotional growth, they can become integrated, responsible, happy human beings. They can begin to experience feelings of calmness, joy, and self-worth.

The following are some brief examples of how I have used some of these techniques with children.

CLAY

The malleability of clay makes it a perfect medium for expression and serves many useful purposes. It allows for kinesthetic and tactile experiences. Here is an example of one session and one way to use clay.

I distributed a sizable piece of clay to each child in a group therapy setting. After some time to experiment with the clay without instructions, I asked the children to close their eyes and follow my directions. (Many children have difficulty keeping their eyes closed—I generally suggest that they allow themselves to peek anytime they need to and then to close their eyes again.) I said things like, "Feel your clay—is it smooth? Rough? Hard? Soft? Is it bumpy? Is it heavy? Light? Cold? Wet? Dry?" I gave them some moments to become acquainted with their piece of clay. Then to further enhance their sensitivity to it as well as to improve their repertoire of things one can do with clay, I said, "Squeeze your piece of clay, pinch it, smooth it, stroke it, poke it, slap it, punch it, bore a hole in it and come out the other side, tear it apart, put it back together, roll it, pat it, make it high, make it flat. What else can you think of to do? Can you make lines in it, bumps, little holes? Will you use your fingernails, fingers, knuckes, palms, elbows? Can you control the clay? Does it control you? Does it want to go its own way? Can you let it do that?" Between each direction I allowed a few seconds. "Try some of these ways of being with your clay and see what you like to do and what you don't like to do. When you are through experimenting, make something with your piece of clay with your eyes closed so whatever you make will be a surprise to you." Each child was asked to describe their object as if it were themselves.

Jimmy (Age eleven): I am an ashtray. I have a smooth bottom and a ledge all around me. I have two places on each side to hold cigarettes. I have some rough places and scratches on me.

Me: Jimmy, who uses you?

Jimmy: My father.

Me: Well, how does he use you?

Jimmy: He drops ashes in me and then he smashes the cigarettes into me to put them out.

Me: Does this fit into your life as Jimmy in any way?

Jimmy: (Voice rising) Yes! That's what he does to *me*. He smashes me—he grinds me like a cigarette.

Me: Would you like to share more about that with us?

Jimmy nods and begins, for the first time in the group, to tell us about his perception of his relationship with his father and his feelings of not being understood. He begins to cry. The other children softly enter into the discussion, sharing some of their own experiences and indicating a good understanding of what Jimmy is experiencing. At a certain point I thank Jimmy for sharing his feelings with us and I know by the calm look on his face that he has come another step toward wholeness and maturity. In this episode it emerged that what was foreground for Jimmy in his life now was his strained relationship with his father. I might have focused in on Jimmy's statement about having rough places and scratches on him as an ashtray. I could have asked him to continue to give his ashtray a voice and elaborate on those rough places, bringing the content into his real life situation. My guess is that the foreground would have been the same. Jimmy was able to get in touch with his feelings easily as he talked. He allowed himself to cry in front of the group and identify his feelings of sadness about his father and himself. At later sessions Jimmy was able to further verbalize and intensify his feelings of anger toward his father, something that frightened him for a long time. He talked about his "ideal" father, the father he wished he had. He found out how he provoked his father, what he wanted from him, how he could begin to get what he wanted and needed without manipulation and through authenticity.

Another example from this session:

Sheila (Age eleven): I am a sun. I am flat. I have two eyes and marks all over my face. I like the sun because it is warm and makes things shine. I have a smiling face.

Me: Sheila, will you say what you said again and every time you said "sun" say "me" instead?

Sheila: I like me because I am warm and make things shine, and I have a smiling face on me.

Me: Does any of what you have said have anything to do with you in your life as Sheila?

Sheila: Well, yes. Sometimes I can make things—people—feel warm. Sometimes I feel shiny and warm. I'm smiling because I feel good now. I really liked the clay. But I don't always smile. Most of the time I don't feel like smiling. (At this point Sheila's facial expression changes, her shoulders hunch up, and she avoids eye contact with me and the others in the group.)

One of the other children asks Sheila what kinds of things make her feel like not smiling. She looks up at all of us and begins to tell us about some of her difficulties with friends, teacher, siblings, and parents. Everyone is now listening intently and I indicate my interest in what she says by reflecting back to her my perception of her feelings from her voice tones. Sheila nods vigorously as I do this, and I can see that she is feeling listened to, accepted, understood—essential ingredients for her therapeutic growth. I then ask her what some of the things are that make her smile and she talks about these, bringing herself back into the room and her experience with the clay. Sheila found much joy in working with the clay, as her shiny face and broad smile now indicate. Sheila had many conflicts in her life. She worried a great deal about everything, always expecting the worst. Beginning with this session and through many others, she has since learned to cope with some of her very real conflicts. She has learned to enjoy the good things in her life as they are happening, rather than ruin these good feelings through her gloomy forecasts of the future. She has come to understand something about the polarities of her existence and her own feelings. She knows now that if she feels angry or sad she can allow herself to accept her own feelings, knowing that at other times she feels calm and happy. She is now able to experience her joyful moments as well as her miserable ones without fear.

Another example:

Joe (Age twelve): I didn't make anything.

Me: You have something there. Just describe what it is, as it is.

Joe: (Stares at his piece of clay for a moment) It's just a lump of nothing. I'm a lump of nothing. And that's the way I feel most of the time—like a lump of nothing.

Me: And now? How do you feel now?

Joe: Right now I feel like a lump of nothing.

Me: You feel like you're not worth much.

Joe: That's right, I'm not.

Me: Thank you for sharing that with us, Joe. I feel very appreciative of you for doing that.

Joe: (Slight smile) That's *ok*.

What is evident here is Joe's low self-esteem, which he openly shared with us. In doing so—making his verbal statement of his existence in life through his own perception—I believe Joe made a giant step toward renewed selfhood. Much of his art work repeated this theme. His drawings were often dominated by large blank spaces, or tiny black and white shapes. Through the techniques described in this paper, Joe began to reveal much of his inner self. As he did he was able to recognize his "put myself down" stance. At one session the statement, "I didn't draw anything here because I wanted it to be perfect and I didn't know how to do that," popped out of his mouth. I asked him to tell us how he would be if he, Joe, could be a perfect boy. He told us some of his self-expectations and began to see, from the feedback of the other children in the group as well as through dialogue with his own more realistic side of himself, that these expectations were pretty unrealistic. I asked Joe to get up and play-act and exaggerate the "perfect" Joe. Joe enjoyed doing this immensely and eventually laughed so hard he could no longer stand up. He began to understand that when he had been criticized for anything by his parents or teacher or anyone, he had (as young children do) swallowed these criticisms whole and had generalized them to all aspects of his being. He began to see that he expected himself to be perfect in order to avoid any criticism or failure. Since this was an impossible task, he remained blank, nothing, and worthless in his own eyes, as well as, he thought, in everyone else's eyes. Little by little Joe began to experiment, explore, try new things, take some risks, and experience the value of his own individuality. He practiced—with encouragement from the group—"chewing up" what others (especially his parents) said about him or in fact about anything, and found that he could reject that which he disagreed with or didn't fit for him, and that he could accept that which was applicable in his opinion. Further, he learned to do this with dignity and appropriate behavior. He learned to state his own position in his life—to take his own stand—thus gaining much respect from others as well as from himself to himself. Needless to say, the other children in the group grew through Joe's struggle.

DRAWING MATERIALS (crayons, pastels, felt pens, pencils, paints, etc.)

After a guided fantasy trip in which I took the children through woods, up a mountain, and into caves where they found doors through which each could enter to discover his or her own particular place, the following was a result:

Linda, age thirteen, drew a picture of a bedroom which included a bed, a table, a chair, three dogs standing and a picture of a dog on the wall. Linda described her picture and the others asked questions such as, "What's that for?" I asked Linda to choose something in the picture she would like to pretend to be. She chose the dog in the picture on the wall. I asked her to be that dog and talk as if it had a voice and could speak works.

Linda: I wish I could come off this wall and join you other dogs playing on the floor.

Me: How does it feel to be up there on the wall?

Linda: I feel lonely—all alone. I don't like watching those dogs play.

Me: Do you, Linda, ever feel that way?

Linda: Yes. That dog is really me. I'm always on the outside.

Me: How about here in this group?

Linda: Yes I feel that way here too. But not as much as I used to.

Me: What do you think made it a little better here than it used to be?

Linda: (Very thoughtfully) Well, I'm doing something. I haven't just been sitting here like a dog on a wall.

Another time I asked the children to create on paper their worlds just using shapes, lines, colors, curves. First I asked them to close their eyes and visualize this world and place themselves somewhere in that world.

Tommy, age nine, colored in a series of curves that looked like hills, and made an enormous, smiling sun coming out from behind the hills. He was a little dot behind a dark hill at the bottom, he told us. Some of the hills were brightly colored and some were dark. He used a combination of felt pens, pastels, and crayons.

Tommy: I'm way at the bottom of the hills and I have to climb them. It's not easy to do. Some of the hills are nice and some are hard. I can rest on some of the hills and play too. I'm trying to get to the top where the sun is. It will take me a long time.

This kind of expression contains fruit for much productive work. The drawing itself tells much about what goes on inside of Tommy. I am forever moved by the depths of feeling and insight that young children express. In working with Tommy and his drawing, I might ask him to elaborate about each of his hills, how he experiences himself as a small dot behind a hill, what it's like to be the sun, or have a conversation between the dot and the sun.

In my experience with children I find that they generally respond easily to fantasy work as well as to taking the parts in a dramatic scenario. Occasionally, a child is resistant or embarrassed or so closed that he or she is unable to freely let go into the realms of imagination. When this happens I deal with the particular child in the manner I deem most appropriate for him or her. I may merely say, "I know this is hard or silly! Would you do it anyway." Or the child may need to experience the kind of activities that may help to free his imagination. This might be accomplished through the use of water play, sand, clay, plasticine, a chalk board, music, finger paints, scribbling techniques, body movement, breathing and relaxation exercises, easy-to-do imagination exercises presented in very small segments, and a variety of games. I might deal directly with the fear behind the resistance or the projection behind the embarrassment. Or I might just allow the child to decide when he is ready to risk something that is difficult and different for him. As the children begin to express themselves easily through the fantasy material and the varied types of expressive projections, I then attempt to gently guide them back into the reality of their lives—having them re-own the parts of themselves that they have exposed—in order to help them begin to feel a new sense of self-identity, responsibility, and self-support. This is difficult for many children, and I may need to approach this task with much gentleness and patience.

SAND

I find sand to be an almost ideal medium in working with children of every age. For my purposes, I purchased a bag of fine white sand at a toy store and poured it into a square plastic footbath which sits on a low table. A plastic runner under the table catches any spillovers of sand. Sometimes I ask children to choose any items they wish for making a scene in the sand and then to tell me a story about it or enact the scene by moving the items or figures around. Sometimes I choose the pieces in order to focus in on a particular situation. On shelves there are baskets containing doll figures, furniture, cowboys and Indians, medieval knights, all kinds of animals, army men, cars, airplanes, boats, small blocks, building, trees, lichen, shells, and lots more. (One learns to develop an eye for interesting items in dime stores, party shops, garage sales.)

Debby, age seven, lived in a foster home and visited her mother on weekends about twice a month. She was referred to me for her extremely aggressive behavior following each visit. At one session, I asked Debby to enact a visit to her mother in the sand. She selected figures to represent her foster parents, the other children in the foster home, herself, her mother, her small sister who lived in yet another foster home, and even a friend of her mother who picked up Debby and the sister for the visits. She built the respective houses with the small blocks and even set up some rooms using pieces of furniture. She then placed each figure in its appropriate place and, with her doll self, enacted the whole process, from being picked up to arriving back to where she lived. It was obvious to me as I watched that the strain of these visits on Debby was tremendous, though her voice was detached, cool, flippant, and matter-of-fact as she told the story. As I watched the movements of her doll figure self and the amount of emotional and cognitive "shifting of gears" involved, I myself felt exhausted. I voiced my own feelings of tiredness and how I imagined that the doll, and perhaps Debby herself, might feel the way I did just watching the whole business. Debby looked at me intently in the eyes for a few seconds, and as I gazed back at her, her face crumbled, her body sagged, she broke into tears, and crawled into my lap where she sobbed for quite some time. With this new aspect of Debby's visits now out in the open, both to Debby herself and to the adults in her life, we were able to make some changes to improve the situation. Such enactments of real situations in a child's life can also be done without the use of sand quite effectively. I find the sand so appealing to children, however, that it lends itself to freer expression.

I might add here too that this episode is a good example of the importance of paying attention to what is going on inside of me. I have learned to trust and make use of my own feelings and body sensations when I work with adults. In working with children this aspect of the work is even more intensified, for children are sensitive and highly observant. If I pretend to be interested when I am bored, I rarely can fool a child. When Debby looked into my eyes, she knew that I was telling her the truth and that she could put her trust in me.

Julie, age twelve, also lived in a foster home, and she never visited her real parents. Her behavior was characterized as predelinquent. Julie was asked to make any scene she liked in the sand. She worked intently, creating a desert with a few little bushes here and there, a rabbit, a snake going into a hole, and a girl standing on a hill. Julie did not want to tell a story—she merely described her scene to me. She was willing to talk as her desert, and as each figure. In every instance she described bleakness and desolation. When asked if anything she said fit in with anything in her own life, Julie began to talk about her terrible loneliness. As Julie was able to express her deeper feelings in our sessions, her acting-out behavior gradually decreased.

The theme of loneliness is quite prevalent in much of the sand play among children. I have found that children will rarely admit to feeling lonely, and yet who among us can look back into our childhoods and not recognize this feeling. Children who are considered dysfunctional in their environments are especially lonely.

Mark, age nine, enacted many battle scenes in the sand using army men, knights, cowboys. At the end of each scene, one side was always left with one sole survivor who sadly buried his comrades, while the other side celebrated its victory, perhaps burying one or two casualties. When asked which of the figures was him,

Mark would always pick the captain or leader of the winning side. Mark wanted very much to be on the winning side in his life. It took a number of sessions before he was able to "own" this as a wish or want or need—and to to identify with the lonely survivor of the losing team. (At least he still survived!)

The above examples are some of the ways that I use expressive techniques with children. Regardless of which mode I or the child chooses to employ at any session the purpose is the same and the process is always different. My goal is to help the child become aware of himself and his existence in his world. Each therapist will find her or his own style in achieving that delicate balance of directing and guiding the session and going with and following the child's lead.

THE DIVORCE PROCESS

James Cole, M.A.

Relationships are like flowers. There are many growth patterns, and with each cycle a new type of life is discovered. Relationships are entered into with love and expectations. A relationship can often end with hate and hurt. Breaking up can also be the most traumatic event of a person's life.

I am going to address myself to the psychological divorce. This is the same process for those who live together as for those who are married. The pain one suffers seems to be directly equated to the emotional commitment to the relationship.

The societal message many hear is that divorcees are losers. But there is another way to look at divorce. A divorce can be a positive experience. People can learn from their mistakes and go on to lead a life without the restrictions they have been putting upon themselves. It can be a time of growth, of freeing oneself.

Divorce is a step-wise procedure, and the steps are the same for both partners. Sometimes the steps are taken while the couple is still living together, over a period of years, while one is secretly planning a divorce and waiting for when the time is "just right." This person has the advantage of emotional and financial support by the mate while going through the steps. People will live in a dead marital relationship while finishing a degree, until the children are out of school, or until a job opportunity arises.

The men and women I see are usually those who have been left. To these people comes the shock that it is finally over. The decision has been made for them.

This is usually the most agonizing of all of the steps. For some it is a period of total emotional loss, a numb period. Although denying their emotions, they find that other parts of their lives are also meaningless . . . jobs or looking for jobs, or day-to-day tasks such as eating are often left undone or at best forced.

As I see these people come into therapy, usually their bodies are tight and their breathing is very shallow. Once they become aware of the personal process by which they hold back their emotions, and what they are doing to themselves by holding back, a surge of anger or sadness will usually flood their bodies. Periods of sadness or anger may come over them for several days while they are away from my office. I encourage them to continue to let it out and to be aware of how they stop themselves.

Ruth came into my office looking dazed. She said she had been served divorce papers two days ago. She said her husband had gone to work as usual that morning, had come home for lunch as usual. At 2:00 that afternoon she was served. For two days she sat in her house not eating, sleeping rarely, and spending most of her time in daydreaming.

In my office she spoke with a very controlled voice, telling me of their married life. Her breathing was very shallow and her fist was clenched. I asked that rather than tell me, she let her husband be in the room for her and tell him. She continued in her controlled fashion to tell her husband. I pointed out her shallow breathing, asking her to take a few deep breaths. As she did this and continued to talk to her husband, she exploded with rage at him, which then changed to deep sobbing. Her crying and anger continued for the rest of the hour. This stage lasted for two more days at home. When she returned to therapy, she said it had been a bad experience and that she was glad she had finally worked through a great deal of it, and that now she was able to also laugh at times. She said the releasing of her emotions was not as bad as the almost lifeless period of numbness she had experienced immediately after she had been notified of her divorce.

This first step, as well as others, can be lengthened by those who suppress their emotions. People report many ways of avoiding their emotions during this period, such as drinking, drugs, and fantasies.

The next step is one of mourning for the death of the relationship. Most people can intellectually state they are divorced and at the same time deny that the marriage is over. They hang onto the thinnest thread of hope that they will get together with the ex-mate. Emotionally they will not admit they are in fact single, divorced persons.

It is during this period that quite often in therapy a lot of unfinished business is brought out to work on. Quite often, just before the split, one partner has denied or blocked that anything bad was happening to the relationship. After the breakup, a lot of "Now I see what was really happening" awarenesses occur. These pertain not only to the "ex" but also, childhood scenes and parental messages.

Typical of this stage are people working on fear of living alone, mistaken dependencies, single parenting, and love-hate splits with the former spouse. I have also noticed that a person entering this stage with an "I feel sorry for" the ex soon develops intense feelings of anger when it is time to let go. If they begin by being angry, they change to feeling sorry for the ex. This step is usually my clue that they are ready to end the mourning and let go of the dead relationship. This is usually accomplished by saying good-bye to the former partner.

This technique is covered very well by Tobin in *Gestalt Is*. I'll cover it briefly for those of you who are not familiar with it.

Therapist: Are you ready to say good-bye?

Person: Yes. (Usually hesitantly)

Therapist: Will you be in that space and time when your ex left you?

Person: Yes, I can visualize him now going out the front door.

Therapist: Call to him aloud that you have something more to say to him.

Person: Bill, stop. I have something to say.

Therapist: Tell him any appreciations you have for him.

Person: Bill, I appreciate the fun we had during the first part of our marriage.

Therapist: Will you now tell him any resentments you have for him?

Person: Bill, I resent (Angrily) your leaving me without warning me and I resent your not wanting to work things out. You're an S.O.B.

Therapist: Is there anything else you want to tell Bill?

Person: No.

Therapist: Will you tell him good-bye?

Person: (Takes a deep breath) Good-bye, Bill.

Therapist: Was that true for you?

Person: Yes.

Usually there is a silence and then tears of sadness. The mourning is completed and the person is ready to continue the life cycle. This next stage is usually marked by trying on new behaviors; i.e., dating, buying things, starting new life-styles and in general, enjoying themselves.

This is when most people leave therapy. Quite often, though, people have come back to me saying that they didn't feel closure on their divorce, even though they didn't want to go back into the relationship and for the most part were having fun.

Just accepting a new life-style is not the end. There is one more step, a ritual for divorce.

In the continuum from birth to death we have some sort of a ritual connected with each change. Change is highlighted with the exchanging of food, drink, and presents.

Birth, birthdays, graduations, promotions, marriages, and even funerals, all have their rituals. Our society does not provide us with a ritual for divorce, and yet divorce has become a part of the continuum for millions of Americans.

I have found that finding a personal ritual for those wanting to finish the psychological divorce is the final step. Personal rituals may consist of a divorce party, with or without the ex present. I have been to many of these and usually they are fun. There is a lot of toasting to the newly single way of life and a lot of encouraging statements.

There are other types of rituals that I know of: At his divorce party, one man wrote "VOID" across his marriage certificate. Gifts are another form of ritual. One woman, divorced for two and one-half years, (her ex was already remarried, which added to her resentment), was still seeking closure. One of the problems during the marriage had been his drinking. Her ritualistic gift to him was two wine goblets and a bottle of wine. This covered two aspects of her hurt: (1) His drinking, and (2) being remarried (the two goblets). As she gave him the present, she reported that in her head she said, "Now I'm done with him."

When helping someone find a ritual I look for their resistance. This may be a blocked form of hanging on. Usually what a person doesn't want to do is where the form of the ritual is found.

One man had neglected to take his exwife's name off the checkbook. I noticed this when he paid me. He said that he hadn't noticed it, but it would cost him $5.00 to get new checks, and he followed that with, "Even the checkout girls at the store would know that I'm single." When he said this, he became aware of how ridiculous it sounded and went home and tore up the remaining checks. I received a note saying that a tear fell as he tore each check, and that for him this was his ritual.

Often it is obvious to an outsider what the ritual is, but not to the person involved. One woman, a year divorced, was looking for a ritual. She mentioned that it hurt her to even look at her wedding album that was on her coffee table. When I asked her why it was still out she had no answer. She also expressed some concern about going to her parents' home for Christmas, where her wedding picture was hanging with those of her brothers and sisters.

After she removed her wedding album and requested that her wedding picture be removed from the family display, she reported a calmness about herself that she hadn't experienced in a year.

Buying a gift for oneself is also another form of ritual. This works when the gift is one that was forbidden during the marriage. Susan was forbidden to drive a small car, "for safety's sake," while she was married. Trading her Buick in for a Fiat was her ritual.

Sometimes the ritual can take place in fantasy, such as toasting a drink to the death of the relationship. My experience is that because it is an outward sign, the ritual is more powerful.

These rituals do not erase the memories, good or bad, but they do give a sense of closure. The ritual does not take the place of the other steps. It is a celebration of change.

CONCLUSION

In retrospect, this book seems complete and yet incomplete. At the time I prepared it, I felt satisfied. Now, however, I have accumulated quite a bit of new material (and hopefully more wisdom). I also regret that I had to omit a number of chapters dealing with specific applications of Gestalt. I plan to include both my own new material as well as more guest chapters in Volume II.

I hope that the reader has gained an appreciation for the eclectic merging of Gestalt with other approaches. With any single model of therapy, clients are adept at learning a therapist's style and will tailor their responses to "match." When the therapist has access to a variety of styles and techniques, the client's "task" of anticipating the therapist's maneuvers becomes much more difficult, and the client's spontaneous responses are nurtured.

Most importantly, I hope to have shown that respectful attention to the client with a non-judgmental stance is the sine quo non of an effective, growth-producing experience.

CPSIA information can be obtained at www.ICGtesting.com
Printed in the USA
LVOW122028080213

319338LV00001B/9/P